AFTER *MOBY-DICK*

AFTER *MOBY-DICK*

AN ANTHOLOGY OF NEW POETRY

Edited by

Elizabeth Schultz & Kylan Rice

Spinner Publications, Inc.

New Bedford, Massachusetts

The authors are deeply grateful to the Melville Society's Murray Endowment Committee for financial assistance in publishing *After* Moby-Dick: *An Anthology of New Poetry.*

Cover illustration: "Queequeg in his own proper person" by Kathleen Piercefield, 2003; collagraph, monotype, etching, polyester plate lithography, and hand-coloring on paper, mounted on eight canvases, 92" x 40"; courtesy of the Elizabeth Schultz Melville Collection of Art at the New Bedford Whaling Museum, New Bedford, Massachusetts.

Cataloging-in-Publication Data

After Moby-Dick : an Anthology of New Poetry / edited by Elizabeth Schultz and Kylan Rice.
    pages cm
  ISBN 978-0-932027-36-8

I. Sea poetry--Melville, Herman--Authorship poetry. I. Schultz, Elizabeth, editor of compilation.

Dedicated to the poets in our lives

Contents

Moby-Dick: Poetry Into Poetry

Part One

Elizabeth Schultz

In 1970, teaching Herman Melville's *Moby-Dick* at the beginning of my career, I was delighted when one of my students submitted, as his final project, a series of found poems from Melville's novels.[1] Tweaking Melville slightly and titling them himself, he set Melville's prose out in poetic lines and indicated in his "Acknowledgements" the imaginary journals where they might have been published: *Kayak, Poetry Tahiti, Up Against the Whale, Spermaceti Review, Popular Whaling, Cannibal Quarterly,* and *True.* I so admired his selections of found poetry from *Moby-Dick* that I saved them to this day. Other readers, tuned into Melville's poetic sensibility in that novel, might have anticipated my student's choices:

Dream

Two & two there floated
into my inmost soul
endless procession
of the whale & midmost
of them all
one grand
hooded phantom
like a snow hill
in the air.

Ahab

He piled upon the whale's
white hump the sum
of all the general rage & hate felt
by his whole race from
Adam down & then
as if his chest had
been a mortar he
burst his hot
heart's shell upon it.

The Calm

An intense copper calm like
a universal yellow
lotus was
more & more unfolding its
noiseless
measureless
leaves upon the sea.

After Moby-Dick: *An Anthology of New Poetry* is a gathering of poems written between 2000 and 2018 in response to Melville's profoundly poetic novel. It is a testimony to the fact that great poetry becomes a catalyst for more poetry. *After Moby-Dick: An Anthology of New Poetry* features sixty-one diverse and eclectic poems, revised or written by thirty-seven poets since the beginning of the twenty-first century.[2] In a diversity of styles, traditional and experimental, ironic and lyrical, personal and political, comic and tragic, these poems reveal the twentieth century's long tradition of responding poetically to the poetry inherent in *Moby-Dick*.

Although *Moby-Dick* has frequently been identified as "The Great American Novel," although it appears in college courses on the genre of novel, and although it is placed in most bookstores in the fiction category, countless critics, reviewers, and readers—in addition to my my former student and a contemporary Nigerian student[3]—have quickened to the profoundly poetic language of Melville's novel. Following the relatively short period of his life (1846 to 1857) which was devoted to writing his nine novels and several short stories, Melville spent the remaining thirty-four years consciously and conscientiously dedicated to writing poetry and to seeking ways of sharing his poetry through publication.[4] Elizabeth Renker notes emphatically that Melville was "primarily a poet," pointing out how active he was "in the vital culture of poetry circulating at all levels of literacy in the world he lived in."[5]

Moby-Dick, in particular, can be seen among his early works as anticipating this life in poetry. Hershel Parker has observed that among the novel's largely negative early reviews, following its 1851 publication, were comments praising it as containing "genuine poetry," as being "full of poetry," as revealing "philosophy in whales and poetry in blubber." Parker concludes that by the time of *Moby-Dick's* publication, Melville's prose was "genuinely poetic, and at times expressed in lines closely akin to Shakespearean blank verse."[6] Christopher Sten devotes an entire book to *Moby-Dick's* association with the poetic epics created by Homer, Dante, Milton, and Eliot, while David Dowling, deeply attentive while listening to *Moby-Dick* marathon readings and to the distinctive sounds and rhythms of Melville's words, concludes that the novel's power lies in its lyricism: "its rhythms, repetitions, internal rhyme, stresses, vowel sounds, and play of common consonant combinations."[7]

Early poetic responses to *Moby-Dick* generally embrace Melville, the writer himself, acknowledging his death in 1891 and several other of his works. The first known poetic response to *Moby-Dick* appears in a brief section of Robert Buchanan's 1885 tribute to Walt Whitman and other American writers. Buchanan extolls Melville as a "sea-compelling man, / Before whose wand Leviathan / Rose hoary white upon the Lee / With awful sounds that stirred its sleep."[8] In 1891, Arthur Stedman reprinted Buchanan's evocation of the White Whale in his obituary for Melville in *The New York Herald Tribune*. Another English poet, John Payne, responded to *Moby-Dick* with a sonnet in 1905, titled "Herman Melville," proclaiming that no other writer had written so well of "the terrors and splendours of the sea."[9]

In 1925, in the wake of the Melville Revival, Hart Crane, also reacting to Melville's death, wrote a memorable poetic interpretation of *Moby-Dick* in "At Melville's Tomb." Crane's four stanzas, which prompted Harriet Monroe to berate him for his illogic and obtuseness, comprise a taut, lyrical elegy, implicitly for Melville himself, but also explicitly for those drowned souls, mourned by the people of New Bedford in "The Chapel" at the novel's beginning, as well as for the *Pequod's* entire crew, whom Ishmael mourns at the novel's conclusion. However, if Crane grieves in "At Melville's Tomb" for those who drown tomb-less at sea, he also lauds the omnipotent sea in imagery, both terrifying and beatific, its "circuit calm of one vast coil, / Its lashings charmed and malice reconciled."[10]

Other well-known twentieth-century poets continued to acknowledge *Moby-Dick* early in the twentieth century in memorable language. The five stanzas of W. H. Auden's 1939 poem, "Herman Melville" seek to encompass Melville's vision over a lifetime of writing. Auden's great poem celebrates the trajectory of Melville's prose, with *Moby-Dick* underscoring its second stanza and its final stanzas reflecting on "Billy Budd."[11] In powerful imagery, in a few phrases, Auden movingly evokes Ahab, Moby Dick, and Ishmael: "The rare ambiguous monster that had maimed his sex, / The unexplained survivor breaking off the nightmare—."Auden directly counters critical interpretations of either Moby Dick or Ahab as Evil incarnate by asserting at the beginning of his third stanza that "the truth was simple. / Evil is unspectacular and always human, / And shares our bed and eats at our own table." Not only does Auden empathize here with Ahab, but in powerful, compressed lines, he also anticipates Hannah Arendt's concept of "the banality of evil." In 1954, Auden, who judged Donald Hoffman's *An Armada of Thirty Whales* as the winner of the Yale Series of Younger Poets in 1954, must have perceived an echo of *Moby-Dick's* grand armada in Hoffman's vision of an immense pod of sperm whales swimming in glory in his title poem.

Following World War II in 1946, Robert Lowell published his profound elegy, "The Quaker Graveyard in Nantucket." Lowell's seven stanzas begin by eulogizing his cousin, drowned at sea, and move toward grieving for all those lost at sea—sailors, fishermen, and whalers, many of them Quakers. He also grieves for the *Pequod's* crew as well as, significantly, for the whales they slaughtered. In his poem's powerful fifth stanza, Lowell invokes not only the bloody dismemberment of whales during the nineteenth century but also the *Pequod's* final moments when Tashtego nails a red flag to the ship's topmost mast:

The bones cry for the blood of the white whale, . . .
The death-lance churns into the sanctuary, . . .
And rips the sperm-whale's midriff into rags,
Gobbets of blubber spill to wind and weather, . . .
And thunder shakes the white surf and dismembers
the red flag hammered in the mast-head.[12]

Charles Olson's poetic and philosophic response to *Moby-Dick* embraced more than forty years of his life, from the nineteen twenties into the sixties, years which included his capacious and visionary *Maximus Poems* (1960) as well as the dynamic, poetic prose of *Call me Ishmael* (1967). Ann Charters writes, "Olson reads *Moby-Dick* as a poetic statement of the experience of space and the awareness of a human universe that in 1850 was prophecy." She comments further that Olson took "Melville as the subject for a large portion of his most successful work, creating out of the relationship literature of intricate design and profound, prophetic vision."[13] As a mentor at Black Mountain College in the 1950s, Olson impacted young poets such as Robert Creely, Robert Duncan, John Wieners, and Ed Dorn with his vision of Melville. Thus, Duncan, alluding to Olson's sense that all Americans are Ishmaels, imagines himself as Ishmael in the last lines of his 1984 poem, "Bring it up from the Dark": "In the midst of my happiness, the worm / of man's misery coils in my heart. / Dream disclosed to me, I too am Ishmael."[14]

Increasingly, through the second half of the twentieth century, American poets, well-known and lesser known, continued to draw inspiration from *Moby-Dick* to illuminate, corroborate, or discover their own visions, publishing not only numerous single poems but also entire collections of poems based on Melville's novel. They responded to Melville's poetic language as well as to a diversity of themes and characters in *Moby-Dick*, often, during this period, associating Melville's characters with quintessential American archetypes. In two separate poems, written in 1947 and 1970, both titled "Herman Melville," Conrad Aiken sees Melville not only as a god-haunted American frontiersman, but also as the "mariner of the human soul" and as one who grapples with "the Logos in Leviathan's roar."[15] Ben Bellit's "Ditty: Moby Dick at Nantucket" appeared in *The Enemy of Joy* in 1964, and Richard Brautigan published a succinct and snappy, satirical poem related to *Moby-Dick*, titled "The Symbol," in *The Pill vs. the Springhill Mine Disaster* in 1968. If Brautigan's title did not do the job of spoofing literary critics, his personification of Moby Dick as "driving a truckload of sea gulls to San Luis Obispo" and of the whale's proclamation that "Hoffa is a lot better / to us whales than Captain Ahab ever was. / The old fart," would have.[16]

"Bob Dylan's 115*th* Dream" (1965) is an extensive, rambling, satirical folk ballad in which Captain Arab, "riding on the *Mayflower*," tells his crew to "forget the whale": "Let's set up a fort / And start buying the place with beads."[17] In his lecture for the 2016 Nobel Award for Literature, Dylan discusses *Moby-Dick* in detail as one of three literary works which had formed his vision, praising the novel's wild mixture of drama, myth, tall tales, and poetry. He identifies Ahab, in particular as "a poet of eloquence" and extolls the novel as having "quotable poetic phrases that can't be beat."[18] George Cotkin writes that through his hallucinatory, often comic lyrics, Dylan, like Melville, riffs "about the lost promise of America, about how monomaniacal devotion to hunting the white whale and profits leads to ruin. But upon the shards of utopian dreams, artists, be it Melville or Dylan," according to Cotkin, "construct a new vision, an artistic voice that beguiles us."[19]

Contrasting in scope with these satirical ditties and with Dylan's captivating ballad are John Bennett's three volumes of poetry, each drawing comprehensively on *Moby-Dick—The Struck Leviathan* (1970), *Knights and Squires* (1972), and *Beyond the Compass Rose* (1983)—and James Magner's six dark, romantic poems in *The Dark is Closest to the Moon* (1973), each introduced with a quotation from *Moby-Dick*. In his short lyric, "Seeing Things" (1973), Howard Nemerov brings science and poetry together, exploring the deceptive nature of all perceptions by citing Ahab's imperative—"Strike through the mask? you find another mask, / Mirroring mirrors by analogy / Make visible."[20]

In 1970, African-American poet, Robert Hayden, following in the footsteps of novelists Richard Wright and Ralph Ellison, both of whom used *Moby-Dick* for the themes and images of their great novels, *Native Son* (1940) and *Invisible Man* (1952), drew on Melville's novel for his powerful poem, titled with Malcolm X's Muslim name, "El-Haji Malik El-Shabazz."[21] The headnote for the poem, "*O masks and metamorphoses of Ahab, Native Son*," suggests that readers are to understand that as Ahab was up against the White Whale, as a black man and a Muslim, Malcolm X was up against American racism and "Yakub's white-faced treachery." With the exception of Muriel Rukeyser, who read her poem, "After Melville" at a Melville Society conference in 1968, to my knowledge, few women felt compelled to respond to the poetry of *Moby-Dick* with poems of their own prior to the twenty-first century.

From early in the twentieth-century, Spanish language poets, however, resonated with *Moby-Dick*. M. Thomas Inge, writing in 1973, testifies to Miguel de Unamuno's "intellectual and emotional excitement when he read *Moby-Dick*"—an excitement reflected not only in the "copious annotations" in his personal copy of the novel, but also in two short poems written in 1929 in the *Cancionero*, Unamuno's "personal diary, kept in the form of short lyrics." In one of these lyrics, Unamuno wonders at Moby Dick's swimming from the sea to encounter him in the Tormes River of Salamanca. In his other brief, but profound *Moby-Dick* poem, Unamuno observes that Pip, the subject of several contemporary *Moby-Dick* poets, sees "not the face" of God, but his feet, and as God weaves "the fabric of destiny / he saw the truth."[22] Jorge Luis Borges' multi-valanced, lyrical response to *Moby-Dick*, "Herman Melville," appeared in 1976.[23] Drawing on the novel's evocation of the "whale road" in Anglo-Saxon poetry, *The Odyssey*, as well as diverse literature from nineteenth-century New England, Borges explores Melville's ties to the sea and to its whales. Movingly, he imagines, too, that Melville had "longed for and possessed that other ocean, which is Writing." The development of Borges' lyrical poem makes the generalization of his final line—"It is the great book. It is blue Proteus."—both persuasive and wondrous.

With the exception of Bennett's trilogy, mentioned above, most twentieth-century *Moby-Dick* poets responded to Melville's epic novel with single lyrical poems. However, from early in the twenty-first century, several poets began to perceive his novel as an inspiration for not only experimenting with language but also for writing full volumes of poems: Deborah Meadows with *The 60's and 70's: The Theory of Subjectivity in Moby-Dick* (2003), Dan Beachy-Quick with *Spell* (2004), Maxianne Berger with *Winnows* (2016), and Jessica Cuello with *Hunt* (2017).

After Moby-Dick, which contains poems by Meadows, Beachy-Quick, and Cuello as well as by other poets publishing independently, was created following an eight-months' (September, 2015, to April, 2016) national online call for poems, written in response to *Moby-Dick*. Kylan Rice and I, who made the call following the 2015 International Melville Society Conference in Tokyo, selected the poems for *After* Moby-Dick from nearly 100 entries: abundant and astonishing evidence that Melville's novel continues to inspire poets. In comparison to *Moby-Dick* poems of the twentieth century, *Moby-Dick* poems of the past nearly twenty years reflect a stunning diversity—not only in the backgrounds of their authors, but above all in their subject matter and in their stylistic experimentation. While it is apparent that very few women poets responded to *Moby-Dick* in the past,[24] among the thirty-seven poets in our anthology, sixteen are women. No longer can *Moby-Dick* be regarded as a boy's book. The poets in *After* Moby-Dick also reflect a diversity of ethnic backgrounds, and they come not only from Nigeria but also from all regions in the United States, Hawai'i to New England, with many of them located in the Middle West. They are all ages. *After* Moby-Dick belongs to the nation.

However, it is the astonishing diversity of subject matter and of poetic styles in *After* Moby-Dick: *An Anthology of New Poetry* which distinguishes and differentiates these poems from twentieth-century poetry written in response to *Moby-Dick*. Included in both sections of the anthology, "Re-Presenting *Moby-Dick*" and "Re-Incarnating *Moby-Dick*," are traditional balladic poems, erasure poems, prose poems, visual poems, haiku, poems in several voices, as well as diverse and astonishing experimental poems which prompt readers to probe Melville's novel in new ways. While poems in our sub-sub library often focus on a chapter, a single episode, or a particular character in *Moby-Dick*; none is generically titled, "Herman Melville" or "*Moby-Dick*" as was the case in the past. Consequently, it proved possible to arrange the poems in both sections of our anthology in an order comparable to the ordering of chapters in *Moby-Dick* itself. Thus, both sections begin, as does Melville's novel with an Etymology and conclude with poetic evocations of the novel's ending.

However, the two sections of the anthology are organized to offer readers two different ways of approaching the novel poetically. "Re-Presenting *Moby-Dick*" aligns poems with chapters, events, and characters in the order in which they are set forth in the novel, elucidating Melville's or Ishmael's perspective. These poems encourage readers to experience the novel as it occurs in nineteenth-century time and space. However, the poems in "Re-Incarnating *Moby- Dick*" bring Melville's chapters, events, and characters into our very contemporary lives; these poems become embodied in ourselves in the process of contemplating, reading, or writing about *Moby-Dick*. Using language in startling and adventurous ways, re-examining familiar and unfamiliar scenes, characters, phrases, and images, the poems in both sections of *After Moby-Dick: An Anthology of New Poetry* prompt the poetry, the philosophy, the narrative, and the images in Melville's novel to come alive anew.

Notes

1. Stephen Bunch graduated from the University of Kansas in 1970 and went on to edit a poetry journal, *Aux Arcs*, and to write very accomplished poetry himself.

2. The two poems by Everett Hoagland included in this collection, "On Johnny Cake Hill: A Sonic Vision" and "Calling Names: Margin Notes," were both written in the 1970s; however, Hoagland has revised and re-published both of these poems in recent publications. "Calling Names: Margin Notes" was first published in *Scrimshaw* (Patmos Press, 1976) and "On Johnny Cake Hill: A Sonic Vision," which was written in 1973, was first published in *This City & Other Poems* (Spinner Publications, 1999).

3. Robert Wallace, Regent's Professor at the University of Northern Kentucky, who for many years has taught a class on Melville and the arts, introduced us to Onyinye Miriam Uwolloh's work. Writing a haiku for every chapter of *Moby-Dick* and using pidgin for her verses, Uwolloh brings international poetry and linguistic traditions together in her poetic interpretation of Melville's novel.

4. Melville's poetry includes *Battle Pieces and Aspects of the War* (1866); the monumental epic, *Clarel: A Poem and Pilgrimage in the Holy Land* (1876); *John Marr and Other Sailors* (1888); *Timoleon* (1891); as well as *Weeds and Wildings with a Rose or Two*, which appeared posthumously. See Douglas Robillard, ed., *The Poems of Herman Melville* (Kent, OH: Kent State University Press, 2000).

5. Elizabeth Renker, "Melville the Poet in the Postbellum World" in *The New Cambridge Companion* to Herman Melville (New York: Cambridge University Press, 2014) 127, 129.

6. See Hershel Parker, *Melville: The Making of the Poet* (Evanston: Northwestern University Press, 2008) 20-21.

7. See Christopher Sten, *Sounding the Whale: Moby-Dick as Epic Novel* (Kent, OH: Kent State University Press, 1996; and David Dowling, "Conclusion: In and Beyond *Moby-Dick*" in *Chasing the White Whale* (Iowa City: University of Iowa Press, 2010) 189-212.

8. Buchanan, "Socrates in Camden, with a Look Around," *The London Academy*, 693 (15 Aug, 1885) 102-103. Reprinted in Stedman, *New York World*, (11 Oct 1891) 26, and Hershel Parker, ed. *The Recognition of Herman Melville* (Ann Arbor, MI: University of Michigan Press, 1957) 121. I am grateful to John L. Marsh's check list of "Verse in Celebration of the Life and Art of Herman Melville" [*Melville Society Extracts*, 14 (April 1973) 3-6] for providing the titles of numerous early poetic responses to Moby Dick.

9. Parker, Ibid. 62.

10. Hart Crane, "At Melville's Tomb," *The Complete Poems and Selected Letters and Prose of Hart Crane*, ed. Brom Weber (New York: Liveright, 1966) 34.

11. Auden discusses Moby Dick's importance to him at length in *The Enchafed Flood, or The Romantic Iconography of the Sea* (1950) in *The Complete Works of W. H. Auden: Prose, 1949-1955*, ed. Edward Mendelson (Princeton: Princeton University Press, 2008) Vol III.

12. Robert Lowell, *Collected Poems* (New York: Farrar, Straus and Giroux, 2003) 17.

13. Ann Charters, *Olson/Melville: A Study in Affinity* (Berkeley, CA: Oyez, 1968) 45.

14. Robert Duncan, *Groundwork: Before the War* (New York: New Directions Publishing, 1984).

15. Conrad Aiken, *Collected Poems* (Oxford: Oxford University Press, 1970) 860-61, 960-61

16. Richard Brautigan, *The Pill vs. the Springhill Mine Disaster* (San Francisco: Four Seasons Foundation, 1968) 95.

17. Bob Dylan, *Lyrics (1962-2001)*, (New York: Simon & Schuster, 2004), 148.

18. The other two works are *All Quiet on the Western Front* and *The Odyssey*. "Bob Dylan-Nobel Lecture." Nobelprize.org. Nobel Media AB 2014. Web. 6 Jun 2017. <http://www.nobelprize.org/nobel_prizes/literature/laureates/2016/dylan-lecture.html>

19. George Cotkin, *Dive Deeper: Journeys with Moby Dick* (Oxford: Oxford University Press, 2012) 254.

20. Howard Nemerov, *The Western Approaches* (Chicago: University of Chicago Press, 1977) 479-80.

21. Robert Hayden, *Words in the Mourning Time* (New York: October House, 1970) 56.

22. M. Thomas Inge, *Melville Society Extracts*, 16 (November 1973) 3-4.

23. "Herman Melville" appeared, translated by Stephen Kessler, in *Borges' La Moneda de Hierro (The Iron Coin)*. In the "Prologue" for his translation of Melville's "Bartleby, the Scrivener," Borges comments in general on *Moby-Dick's* impact: "Page by page, [*Moby-Dick*] expands, to the point of usurping the magnitude of the cosmos . . . the symbol of the whale is less apt for suggesting that the universe is vicious than for suggesting its vastness, its inhumanity, its bestial or enigmatic stupidity . . . *Moby-Dick* is written in a romantic dialect of English, an impassioned dialect that alternates or combines rhetorical schemes of Shakespeare and Thomas De Quincey, of Browne and Carlyle" (http://www.tanfonline.com/doi/abs/10).

24. In the list of poets identified in the checklist compiled in 1973 by John L. Marsh for the *Melville Society's Extracts* [14 (April 1973) 3-6], three women's names appear in a list of thirty-one.

Moby-Dick: Poetry Into Poetry

Part Two

Kylan Rice

The poem remembers what the world was like before there was language. Before an "I" could account for itself and for its milieu, calling it all by name. Language, lyricized, develops its own musics and logics, its own syntaxes, puts the pleasure of the tongue before the prosaic sensibility of rational mind. The poet gives herself over to the mastery of meter, rhythm, pun, assonance, and the recombinant play of words, which become autonomous and organic within the frame of the poem, reconstituting the world which was first and indestructibly constituted when we were taught to make sense of it by ordering it, by calling it by name, calling it *bottle*, calling it *ball*, calling it *Ishmael*.

Moby-Dick is as much a poem as a novel because it knows that language has the power to world by unworlding then reworlding, heaving out colossal orbs. The poet dives into language, into its wondrous vented depths, and loses himself in the ensuing collapse where water and firmament become one again, as they were on creation-day. This celestial thought, a first thought, a thought before all thought, sounds like madness when it is spoken to human ears. It sounds like poetry.

To lose yourself is to remember that you are not only yourself, no isolato nor insular Tahiti. Ishmael begins his account as an individual differentiated by names and language—"Call me Ishmael"—but as the novel runs its course, there is less and less of Ishmael to be found. While the first image of the novel is of a person and a name, the final image of *Moby-Dick* is of the sea, vast and indifferent and undifferentiated, rolling on even as it rolled five thousand years ago.

And yet, to begin his tale, Ishmael asks—he demands—to be identified. His name must first be uttered on another's tongue. Ishmael supplicates in order to effect his own summoning. Like every "I," he requires a "You." Already he is entangled in whale-lines. This is what a poem knows.

After Moby-Dick is a sub-sub library of poetry that attempts to foreground the essentially poetic nature of Melville's novel. It does so in deeply considered ways, mapping and remapping the relationship of Self to Other—the fundamental drama of the lyric poem—and turns and returns to the ground of Melville's language just as poets in their work are turned and returned to the grounds of language itself so as to speak what they see: the coral insects, God's foot on the treadle of the loom.

Near the beginning of the collection, we are tuned by Dan Beachy-Quick to the ways in which the work of assembling an anthology might resemble the same work of speaking the poem, speaking the I, which is always already anthologized or choral:

I

am editor, I
    fathom depths
    not my own—I
Own nothing
But some other's page, Author Unknown.

These lines describe an economy of intervention and interrelation upon which editing and authoring are founded. Beachy-Quick's poems, excerpted here from a book-length treatment of *Moby-Dick* titled *Spell*, overlay the world and narrative structure of Melville's novel onto the world of a reader—any reader—who reads and writes about *Moby-Dick*. Beachy-Quick's poems turn the work of reading and writing into a work of pursuit, prosecution, and epic risk.

Later, Beachy-Quick will address his reader as an editor, insisting as an author, "Sir, these bound pages / Are bound for you." In such a formulation, the book in which the Same witnesses to their self is essentially bound or made on behalf of the Other. Further, by foregrounding the editorial stage of the writing and reading process, Beachy-Quick's poems demonstrate how a text, written or read, is never finished, but leaves its copestone ever to posterity: "Sir, when my book arrives, when each page / You've untied lets go the breath it held / That was my breath, then breath will not be mine . . ." Here, Beachy-Quick raises the stakes even higher: readers are not only editors; in fact, the very breath the reader draws is a re-breathing, a breath transmitted to them by others, the Other who is an author. "Source is source / of breath," Beachy-Quick writes in a line that summarizes the aims of this anthology of poems: to witness to the ways in which the work of reading and writing is open, porous, continuous, invoked by and invocational of others.

Ivan Klein and Douglas Storm have each also offered innovative models of lyric subjectivity with respect to others. Speaking as through Ishmael, Klein's poem, beginning with the word "You," clarifies the deep relationship that exists in *Moby-Dick* between the novel's main character and his audience, emphasizing the ways in which both poem and novel are, in essence, works of witness, testament. Storm reintroduces us to the stone cenotaphs or tablets that adorn the interior of Father Mapple's chapel in New Bedford, signaling how this scene forecasts the increasingly slippery distinction between "I" and "We"—between private self and public body, especially the body reduced to inscription and made public postmortem—which builds over the course of Melville's novel. In his concluding stanza—"bodiless (turned) / into (under) better being / (un) bodied into / not me"—Storm dramatizes the function of the memorial, which turns death into a banner under which the living gather in their shared fate.

Indeed, one of the curious discoveries of this anthology is how assiduous the poets writing after *Moby-Dick* are at recognizing and harnessing the polyvocal nature of the novel. Just as Melville toggles freely among the voices of the crew, of Ishmael, of Ahab, the writers in this collection variously speak through the masks of these personae, too. Onyinye Miriam Uwolloh not only channels Ishmael's voice into haiku form, she additionally transposes his account into pidgin English, spoken as though to the multinational crew of the *Rachel*, who rescue the sole castaway of the Pequod's wreck. Uwolloh's revelation is to remind us that *Moby-Dick* is a story that has been, and continues to be, told and retold—a pliant narrative of witness that was always already adapted, formulated through a hybrid voice to an audience of many tongues; a narrative whose main concern, despite its intricacies and troubled opacities, is comprehensibility, to be both comprehended and comprehensive at once.

With Uwolloh's work as an exception, it may also be worth reflecting on reasons why Ahab and Moby Dick are among those "characters" most commonly vocalized in these pages. While the relationship between Ahab and the Whale ostensibly comprises the content of the entire novel, in Melville's text, both figures remain curiously out of reach both to Ishmael and his audience. Given this psychic distance, several poets in this anthology seek to further illuminate the foot- and handholds that may help grasp the motives and minds of Ahab and his quarry. Using the voice of the whale as framework, Jessica Cuello's poems negotiate the intimate boundaries between exteriors and interiors of all kinds, casting the (female) skin as a threshold, exploring the violence of eros that burgeons and beats between lovers, between selves and others in inextricable states of entanglement. Like Cuello, Devon Balwit uses Ahab's persona as a *camera obscura*, lighting the disturbing yet intimate cycles of obsession and fidelity lurking in amorous as well as cetalogical contexts.

In "Ahab, to His Wife," David Kann elaborates on Ahab's other "bond and covenant," sounding the deep marital prehistory to Ahab's more visible monomania. Kann's is a witness to the accretion—as if a kind of ambergris—of solitude and self that can occur even within the close twoness of marriage. The problem of the self shows itself here: even in the midst of the fondest memories of his beloved, Kann's Ahab is yet "self-gaffed dragging avid death" behind him. Cuello returns to further plumb this dilemma in "Chapter 92: Ambergris," describing the curious internal formations that happen inside speakers that both exposes them to and makes them valuable to the desirous prosecutions of others.

Used and reused, then, as a paradigm for understanding deep, inextricable relationships, the channeled voices of Ahab and the Whale offer this anthology's poets a framework with which to understand the primordial eros of relationality. Desire is at issue here, and at issue especially in work by Rachel Richardson, whose poems explore the ways in which understanding desire might help us understand the world and the ways we represent the world to ourselves and to others. Much like Melville's chapter by the same name, Richardson's poem "Of Whales in Paint; In Teeth; In Wood; In Sheet-Iron; In Stone; In Mountains; In stars" tries to pierce through the objects of desire to recover desire as an object in itself ("Desire, if ever found, / if ever hauled up with a deep hook / and stripped / of its algae and rust . . . "), but the effect ultimately shows how nothing is "in service / of itself"; that objects are desires and desires are in a constant state of phenomenological flux, nothing ontological beneath the surface of the ontic. Desire, which structures human experience of the world, is always for something or someone. It is never abstract.

At the center of this intersubjective and joint-stock cosmography is that first principle of experience, of radical encountering: the body. The body is known here as a microcosm of the ever-juvenile universe itself, appearing and reappearing as the medium of voice and of poem. "Skin remains a question," Deborah Meadows reminds us, exploring the ways in which the body's properties are as transitive as other hunks of matter, much like Lee Upton's ambergris, which, though loosed in time, world-roaming, still returns to dab as perfume "right there / behind a small human ear"—a gesture that likewise returns us from the kind of wild, ranging, recombining speculation that ambergris affords back to the intimate locationality of the body.

The body is the framework for experience, but also a means of experiencing others and otherness, exposing us to the reality of those others. This idea finds voice in Nicholas Spengler's poem "Articulation," in which the body becomes a reminder there is no sole existence, no mono-minded monad:

> I dreamed I was an island
> insular and alone,
> lost in latitudes unknown—
>
> Or a whale in the arctic,
> warm-blooded citadel
> in an empire of ice;
>
> But I awoke in your arms
> snug—a spark
> in winter's hyperborean heart
>
> And I felt myself melt in you . . .

Touch—and touching others—becomes a principle not of surface, contact, and buffer, but of dissolution, intermarrying, blending.

But it is too easy—and Melville knows this, as do the poets who "walk in [his] shoes / around Manhattos" (Ivan Klein)—to make simple claims for intersubjectivity, forgetting the mediated complexities of the relationship between Self and Other. These poems offer systems and describe apparatuses for understanding the continuous process of re-presenting and re-incarnating that limns the interval between one being and another. In Jeffrey Yang's short poem, to "wheel" around the white whale is to find the self "freed / from ego"—which is not to say the self is destroyed or swallowed up, but rather changed, or disarticulated from itself. A self without ego is still a self, though it may be more vulnerable to or discoverable by others. That being said, the reverse is not always true. In *Moby-Dick*, the character

Bulkington can be read as an instantiation of the elusiveness of the Other, pursued though he is by his shipmates. Louis Phillips revisits this figure in a series of poems that reflect on the interpersonally and socially constructed nature of subjective experience. Despite the best intentions and attempts of a poem that seeks to "Conjure him, voodoo him, / Swivel the Book of the Dead," Phillips concludes that "Someone is missing. / Someone is no longer here"—a conclusion that ripples and resurfaces across the murky and sinister social swamp that his poems inhabit. In "Enveloped in Whale Lines," Michalle Gould articulates further the consequences that accompany attempts to conjure or voodoo the Other using representational means: "here is a rifled heart, half-unhinged / by the visible absence of the whale; bare words and facts cannot sustain / his vision of that beast." Regardless of the intensity of the desire for presence, which takes shape here as Ahab's fervent, raging quest for the presence of his elusive White Whale, Gould witnesses to the failure of "words," "facts," and other representations ("this mortar will not clamp to the surface, / it has no stick to it") to instantiate "the very thing"—or any person, as the case may be.

And yet, caught in the monkey-rope, bound up within and fated by the networks of desire that enmesh us to one another, we are obliged to represent the Other in the same breath as we witness to ourselves. Take Adam Day's "Pip," which reflects on the ways in which the othering nature of racialized looking inscribe and re-inscribe and ultimately doom us to the cyclic violence of racial difference. And recall again that Ishmael had to invoke a listener before he could name himself and begin his tale—which, in the end, is not so much *his* tale as it is the tale of some other man's implacable will and want. Not only is there no way to say "I" without also saying "You," Ishmael cannot speak about his own story without witnessing Ahab's. Elizabeth Schultz acknowledges this dilemma in "Ishmael's PTSD," where she re-narrativizes Ishmael's story as a means of underscoring the ways in which Ishmael's telling—and, indeed, all writing—is an act of witness. Of Ishmael, Schultz writes,

> . . . In time,
>
> reaching the Arsacides, he witnessed,
> with equal eye, the weaving of life's
> green tendrils with death's white bones,
>
> and at last, grasping the ungraspable
> he wrote it.

In this poem, Schultz adopts the position that Ishmael held with respect to Ahab. She observes the trauma an Other has suffered and—less in spite of the difficulties of this kind of witnessing, but because it is unavoidable, as unavoidable as the green regrowth of foliage in the midst of death in the Arsacides—she writes it. Witness begets witness. As Rick Mitchell puts it, "An image is unhinged by yet another image."

Images and "copies," Mitchell shows, mediate and multiply experience. Other meditations on mediation abound in this anthology. Sylvia Cavanaugh uses W.B. Yeats as a lens by which to rethink the encounter between Ahab and Moby Dick. Schultz uses *Moby-Dick* as a frame-text for thinking through her experience sailing on board the *Morgan*, the world's last whaling vessel. My own poems sing in response to Dan Beachy-Quick's song of response to Melville, whose novel relays its own echolocations, *mise en abîme*. In "Whale Watching," Anthony Caleshu uses the epistemology of, and his identity as, a reader to try and grasp the formation of bonds between a father and his newborn child. Just as desire cannot exist in abstraction, untethered from the real, neither can knowledge. Knowledge-building happens *through,* through a mediating apparatus, whether that is our embodied experiences or the embodied experiences of others, by whom we are embodied. Knowledge is a form of empathy. *Moby-Dick* knows this. The essential nature of the poem knows this. William Orem knows this in "Whale, Cape Henlopen," whose speaker, on encountering a beached whale identifies and resonates with that whale on the basis of the whale's corporeal and anatomical capacities for resonance:

> We still could see
>
> the gentle rest of hip in spine,
> a treasury of scattered vertebrae.
>
> And something of the jaw, wherein
>   they say the music lies—
>
> that long, expressive arc,
>
> like us, that sings.

Take that final line alone. Take the empathic revelation of its first clause: "Like us"—*that* sings. *Like us.* That is song. That is poetry.

An anthology of poetry written after *Moby-Dick*, then, is not just any mere anthology. The result in *After* Moby-Dick is a profound meditation on the ways in which the nature of this novel and the nature of poetry and the nature of anthologizing all reveal each other. Much like the whale ship, a poem is an apparatus of lines, of whale-lines and monkey-ropes, stretched tight as harp-strings, binding self and other, reader and writer, in destinies that cannot be disentangled. Because the fate of destiny is not a hero's alone. Fate is shared. Our fate is other people.

Re-Presenting *Moby-Dick*

Ishmael

Ivan Klein

You, who come after me, who live
In the sunlight of my shadow;
You who were not cast out
and to whom the world belongs;
With your paid judges and priests–
Where and when did you sign away
Your souls, your spirits–
And for what share of the great ship's
killing profit?
    What laws govern the conduct of the wanderer,
the outcast, the orphan cold and hungry?

Etymology of Whale-Fish and Grace

Danelle Lejeune

That *H.* makes up the significance. Sets it apart from,
Wail—a broken heart or a grieving mother's grace
and *Wale*, the weft of cloth or the mark on my bosom
from the anger I made, a belt in his handsome fist.
The *gunwale* of the ship out in the Savannah harbor,
the rough planking grain of wood, salted upright.
I will not lose myself to slaking seas, drowned and blind—
this cry, swelling up from down there, this place where
only waves have known, the whale-fish and now me—
that unpronounced *H.* swallows ships and regrets and intentions,
tallow under skin for candles we burn end to end sweetly.
Wail, Wale, Whale tangle up on our flesh eating tongues,
taking to sea before I lose myself again and again—
with each breath, I know how much that whispered *H.* is worth.

Etymology of: The Unabridged (*Ishmael Mulls*)

Dan Beachy-Quick

Yes

I am one—a
Mariner who sailed through *midnight*
Sea of milky whiteness: a
                              haunting, I

Found terror—. Blank-dread, dread-
Eyed, *white-lead chapter*, I
Am editor, I

                    fathom depths
                    not my own—I

Own nothing
But some other's page, Author Unknown.

          Drop anchor
          In ink and drop anchor
          In ocean: lead sinks

          But sails in current
          Above no bed
          The anchor is ocean's sail, and

I am one who sailed
Through midnight sea: a

                         sea, a
                         blank

Sea. I suffered so—
Beneath my captain's madness, my own

Book-self abridged
While the ocean-volume in blanks
              ocean   in blanks
                          in
              ocean   blank

I swear (my hand on the surface
Of the moonless ocean's ink) I would surrender

Myself to You
For a typo: <u>a ocean, a ocean</u>
        <u>an sea, an sea</u>

                but one mark, a pip, please
                misspell
                        the empty sea—
                for me, spell wrong, the sea.

Call me Ishmael (again). Call me _____.
                cormorant|ink-winged bibliophile
                albatross|editor-of-distant-wandering
                sea-hawk|ravenous lexicographer

    Let one blue line of the lined page
    Be bed to interlined white
    Expanse of ocean. Ink me in
    The anchor if I need I want
    To need less

The definite article above the unabridged
Blank to define. No. A possesses, it
                is dispossessed. Me—a_____. [inkpot]
                        a _____. [desires a]
                    a me. Editor—

A "You." Take your salt-fraught, crystal-quill, your
Evaporated fathoms
            and mark me, a
            sub-altern, mark me
The godly,
        ungodly article: *a*—
                who is a
                single one? Show him

To me. I'm writing
A dictionary, un-

Abridged. My riddle is:
First Letter, First Entry: *a*. Who is he?

31

Tablets

Douglas Storm

Returning
I sallied
out
upon
my special errand
the sky
changed and charged
drivingly sleeting
stubbornly storming
I fought
and found
and entered
a reigning silence
of sailors wives and widows
congregational
against
grief
stormingly shrieking
insularly sitting
incommunicably
apart

seated
I
pretendingly quoting
They
steadfastingly eyeing
black-bordered
masoned
marbled
tableted
sacredly worded
memorially
lost

We
survivored
overboard
out of sight
off shore
by deeps
lately
emplaced
unrecorded
untellingly
wounded

women
wealing
women
wailing
women
weaving
women
weaning
women
unwilling

bosoms brooding
desolate upon
ungreenly
unburied
unflowered
unleaved
undead
absent ashes

oh
bitterly blank marbles
despairingly inscribed
voids

gnawingly
unbidden
unrisen
secondless coming
ungravenly placed

surely-not

feathering
unfed
hopes
unfloated
upon
unshored
bosomless
deeps

without-meaning

same-fate
be-thine

bodiless (turned)
into (under) better being
(un) bodied into
not me

Queequeg and Ishmael Do It in the Spouter Inn

Rajiv Mohabir

(Erasure poem from *Moby-Dick*)
for Jordan Andrew Miles

I.
Imbedded in the hump
that harpooner eats nothing but steaks,

and likes 'em rare.
Says the Innkeeper of my bedfellow.

I began to feel suspicious
of his peddling head around town

and resolved to spend the rest
of the evening as a looker-on.

Suppose now, he should tumble
in upon me at midnight,

I, a great fish, and he,
a wrinkled Jonah.

II.
A tramping of sea boots in the entry;
the door flung open
and in rolled a wild harpooner.

Seldom such brawn in a man heads
to my bed. I've no idea
of sleeping with a madman,
this harpooner is stark mad—

I got up and took off my shirt, my pantaloons.
Undressed, I tumbled into bed.

He continued the business of undressing,
showed his chest and arms
jumping into bed with me. It's high time
to break the spell in which
I had so long been bound.

I screwed hard my "dark skinned" harpooner,
at ease during these queer proceedings.

Better sleep with a sober cannibal
than a drunken Christian.

III.
I lay, Queequeg's arm thrown over me,
as though I had been his wife.

When I was a child, I well remember
a somewhat similar circumstance
that befell me: sounds of gay voices
all over the house.

Now take away the awful fear.

The night's events soberly recurred
one by one, in fixed reality.

Unlocking his bridegroom clasp
I strove to rouse him,
hugging a fellow male
in that matrimonial style,
I extracted a grunt, quietly eying him.

He treated me with such consideration,
sporting his harpoon
like a marshal's baton.

IV.
You cannot hide the soul.

He made no advances
with the other seamen in the inn.

I felt a melting in me,
drawn towards him. He looked
so pleased, so complimented.

We sat exchanging puffs
from that wild pipe of his.

What is this if not worship:

To do to my fellow
what I would have my fellow
do to me—
this is prayer without ceasing,
that is the will of God?

We undressed and went to bed;
opened the very bottom
of our souls to each other.

V.
Lain thus, Queequeg now
and then throws
his brown legs over mine.

In bed I beg him.

To enjoy bodily warmth,
some small part of you must be cold.

For now I like nothing better
than to have Queequeg
smoking by me.

This experienced harpooner,
intimate with the hearts of whales,

embraces me; presses
his forehead against mine and blows
out the light.

From Nantucket Out

Patrick Pritchett

for John Levi Barnard

O to go out with the captain
who prizes naught but the gnostic
depths, seizing horizon
from a quarter deck
the color of a bleached acorn.
And the hard-born men
who ride with him to sea?
They do rush imperial waves
with a metacentric buoyancy.
The kingdom of breathing is theirs
impossible to reverse
and yet—
they will be dead entire who
finally hold the sea in their mouths
greenwater flashing on deck
souls shipped to a further point
past Sable Island or the Azores
doing lorn business in great waters.
Lordly always
above the crush
he stands well out
scanning from crow's nest
white spray, white miles, white rogue
deluding him, ransacking folly
sweeping open fields of water
from the salted mitre
of his hard-pegged wheel.
And launched upon lost
harborless immensities
a score of lamps washes
his body in black milk
of ship's hull
astral oils as could
singe the air insane off
the Cape of Good Hope
or burn in fissureless
Pacific blue vortex
all worshipful iron
clasp striking
through the cryptic
mask to the wave
beneath the wave.

Ahab and the Whale

Sylvia Cavanaugh

> *"How can those terrified vague fingers push*
> *The feathered glory from her loosening thighs?"*
> "Leda and the Swan," William Butler Yeats

Sudden slip along the tilted wet wood of a whaleboat, how
his legs flew unbidden skyward. Can
this treachery ever seem anything but slow motion in memory? Those
white moments felt from the depth of bowels; his youthful mind terrified.
A whaling life was once just the vague
fancy of a bored schoolboy, counting days on his fingers.
Figures of any kind were not his thing. O, how Father would push.
But no, he was destined to stride across a boat careening atop the
viscous roll of salt-gray oblivion. To be almost feathered
in confidence; to command water. The glory
of a two-legged beast, with lungs, to lord over seas; a glory derived from
the delusion of dominion over fishes. The sleek ship; her
oily industry; all this promise before that endless loosening
grip. Before twin rows of rounded teeth ground to marrow all bone below the thigh.

Meditation on a Broken Leg; or, Mediation Between a Bone and a Missing Bone *(Ahab, after the Carpenter carves him a new leg)*

Dan Beachy-Quick

Cancel me

My debt in the turning lathe's ledger—
I've a hewn leg more narrow in mind

To stand on the jawbone of the jaw
That bit me from my own.

I signed me off on my severed nerve
's electric command: *turn-to, strike top-sail, strike—.*

The pain-whetted mind (*strike—to the Season-on-the-Line*),
The pain-whetted, pulse-forged, blood-bladed mind—

                         I am to you Due
                         I owe, I feel

An air-flesh grown unseen
On this too-much-seen bone

                as if I were
                not a
                vessel half-sparred

I wear a bruised heel on a foot
That has no heel to bruise.

Madness aches me
A step
      further on: *cursed . . . mortal*
                        inter-indebtedness
Which will not do away with ledgers

I know who I owe and who
Owe me: You:
                White
            Whale: a *Sum Unknown.*

Another me

Exists the sun

Cannot know: belly-deep:

I tendon my thought to the Shoreless—
Wave-ridden: at depths, I am

Not-known. To myself

I whisper the white whale's name.
I square my jib into the gale, sail
Where the wind unleashed would not allow me.
When lightning struck the mast
                    the mast was fire-blessed to me—

When a storm-lit, magnet-flame, lit on the blood-forged lance
I took the lance to lip
                    and breathed
The God-flame out. God-like. God-like—

    I know the angle of flame
    At breath's bidding. I know the angle
    Of the sail in wind.

    O, bide on me   source is source
    Of breath   inspire and no other
    No other   lifts this hand my hand
    Into the wind   I palm my sail
    Myself and strike   the God who strikes

Ask me

What is a Captain?

                                 "What is a Captain,

Captain?"

He who fills the White
Ledger with Red Ink.

Ask me how much costs
A *Whaling Profit*? Ask me—

"Faith, sir, I've———."

"Faith? What's that?"

"Why, faith, sir, it's only a sort of exclamation-like—."

                          Ask me to compare:
Within the sun upon the sea
I see
    a darkling self
Who is more me than me.

I feelest tingling life; there, exactly there, there . . . do I.

A tingling life
In the ghost-limb, jawbone, a
Tingling life
           in the jawbone, unutterable—

Is't a riddle? the sun?

          Unknown sum? Light begins in
          A single point, a star.
          And then a star expands into
          A planet, my hand gestures an orbit
          Of light.

          Let it dwindle—if it drowns
          Let it drown
          In the ocean a lamp the sun.

It insults me. Strike the sun.

Chapter 31: Queen Mab

Jessica Cuello

She hath been with me:

my tooth lodged in his leg
swimming through cold spots
where the sun was not
the water black

sleeping   my hand hit your chest
and the blanket bled

your eyes in my eyes and arms
in arms. I beat
you down   and beat against
the door.   I swam, was flying,
was breach. And dove.
Fear was dust. Chase was over, old
and tired. Turned around. Turned face.
Turned rage and strength.
I left water. I grew legs.
I made a raft for the child,
but the men I sank.

Chapter 36: The Quarter-Deck

Jessica Cuello

Beauty is a Pasteboard Mask

you claim, talk of the face

Strike through the mask

mask: skin, sinew, hump, and eye
below the mask: is I, is I

That inscrutable thing is what I hate

It is not a mask: I wear these hands
objects: nose, my crooked jaw

my objects oh me, my life
and object, take me, punch through

my property, take the thought
I swim inside this mask

I think there
Is my inheritance, is patient,

is an ear, take binds
Take never open up, with all broken

take lance and never open
Beauty has no mind she has no mask

You hate because you think
to see is strike, to look beneath

to pierce and see below
You think to break

will open

Chapter 44: The Chart

Jessica Cuello

A graphite
line runs through his skull
and teeth

His eye is pasted to my neck

My mottled body
in his head, my forehead white
beneath the dusk

I always wanted a picture of myself:
a pulse, a tethered eye

I always wanted a man who knew my mind

Too bad the graphite digs
too hard a path,

and nothing's behind the teeth
but teeth

Watchful

Devon Balwit

One more turn around the deck,
the thud of wood on wood, my
obsession plain, like a picked scab
oozing through white linen. The
horizon mocks me—forever
spoutless. I'll bash the teeth of any
tar who laughs. We're all of us
chasing white whales—the lap
of our mams, God's blessing,
the perfect tits, our weight
in gold. Say what you will
in your hammocks at night, butt-
fucking each other until the next
port. Me, I'm faithful to my white
mountain, my white ghost. I save
my spunk for the Spouting One,
scan the waves, know his name,
his ripple, his smallest scar,
know him out there. We'll have
each other sure as sure. His belly
will be my sepulcher or him
my scrimshaw. There'll be no
parlay. Go ahead, snicker, you
pox-scarred bastards, you sots.
What do you know? What do you
know of me? What will you
be known for? Nothing—less
than nothing. Be thankful I've
made you the throwing arms
of my harpoons, the rowers of my
boats, the haulers of my sails. I
will make you watchwords, fill
your nostrils with the sweet stink
of blood, of rendering. Another
turn, another. Let the cabin boy
sleep on in the crow's nest.
When it comes, the call will be
mine, the victory mine. There
he spouts, my hearties! There!
There! There! It's time!

Cetology

Rajiv Mohabir

(Erasure of Chapter 32, "Cetology")

Sperm:
>Most formidable creature of the globe:
>majestic in aspect, most valuable
>
>in commerce, the only creature
>from which spermaceti is obtained,
>
>not being used for light, but only
>as a medicament, and so the appellation.

Hump-Back:
>He has a pack on him like a peddler,
>his oil is not very valuable.
>
>Gamesome and light-hearted,
>he makes gay
>
>and foam and white water.

Sulphur-Bottom:
>A gentleman with a brimstone belly,
>
>he is never chased. Prodigies
>are told of him, Adieu.

*

Right:
>Most venerable of the leviathans,
>multitudinously baptized, the Baliene
>
>Ordinaire whale for more than two
>centuries past has been hunted
>
>by the Dutch and English, long pursued
>in the Indian Ocean.

Killer:
>He is very savage—
>a sort of Feejee fish.
>
>We all are killers on land
>and on sea.

Huzza:

> Something must be done.
> He always tosses himself
>
> to heaven. Full of fine spirit,
> they are lads that live before
>
> the wind. A fine and delicate
> fluid extracted from his jaw
>
> sailors put on their hones.

Black Fish:

> Blackness is the rule among whales.
> His voracity is well known. Mephistophelian
>
> grin on his face, he will yield
> upwards of thirty gallons of oil.

*

Fin-Back:

> Under this head he's reckoned a monster
> in every sea. His great lips are very shy.
>
> He always goes solitary; unexpectedly
> rising to the surface of sullen waters.
>
> If you descend into the bowels of leviathans,
> what then remains of you?

Narwhal:

> Horn mistaken, the creature
> is on the sinister side, analogous
>
> to the aspect of a clumsy left-
> handed man. A piercer, he thrusts
>
> his horn up so it breaks through.

Razor-Back:

> He eludes philosophers
> though no coward. Let him go.

Of Whales In Paint; In Teeth; In Wood; In Sheet-Iron; In Stone; In Mountains; In Stars

Rachel Richardson

I

Desire, if ever found,
     if ever hauled up with a deep hook
and stripped

     of its algae and rust
and sanded down
     and burnished to its new
seawashed sheen
        (a smoothness, an interiority
          exposed)

might save. That lucky ship
     is years gone from the harbor,
no word delivered home
     though the crew
        surely wrote at every port.

Turning away from you
        and you from me
     in our bed, falling into shared

silence in a curtained room
     is perhaps like this,
or perhaps
     nothing like this.

II

Some men carved
        their wives' faces
     into the whales' teeth
they saved
     from the try-pots—

in their bunks
        (their lamps lit
     with spermaceti) they caressed
the horned pearl
     or in fair weather worked
on deck. The slip
        of a finger might make her
a mermaid, leg-line
     curling into a tail—
or give her a child
        clinging to the hem
     of her woolen dress.

III

And looking up at a sky
      without a city
to blunt it

             (I never said
      I was lonely)

is a wonder:
the cetacean world
      cavorts in the heavens.

How to explain the depth

      (I never said it but perhaps
          it still was true)

—the depth of such desire
          not to have a body

at all, but be
      phosphorescent?

          In other words
      be the flame

not pilot light.
      Be fire in service
of itself.

A Brief History of The Whale Fishery

Rachel Richardson

Elbow-deep in the cool white
they flayed into strips, rolling
the winnowing body

as they unraveled her
and the sharks,
smelling their work, circled

and snapped. Unlucky men
hot-stepping the planks.
Lucky men feasting on stars.

Misfits and criminals.
Whittlers, prophets, magicians, boys.
In distress, smothering in fog

or storm, they hoisted mattresses
into the crow's nest
and set them on fire.

Goodbye sleep.
(Melville: *Who are hearsed
that die on the sea?*)

If not the body itself
lit through—
if not the body

they would use
their beds, the brightest thing
to heave—

if not
the body itself
a lighthouse—

the body:
such thin skin
and gold beneath.

Ahab, to His Wife

David Kann

I'd lived too long in a rented room,
barely sleeping in a rented bed.
Outside my single window
a buoy bell bonged in the swells' sway at the slack of the tide.
In the wind I heard whispers of an eternity
of narrow beds and single-dented pillows.
Then you opened to me, my lee harbor.

Here, now, who-knows-where, with the sea fog settling down the sky,
sweet September's smell riding the wind takes me
to our ripeness and the memory of the knot of your heels against my back
and how your arms clenched me to the loamy land and the seasons' swing.
Thinking of you
I imagine warm dark barns and hay-smell
far inland beyond the sound of the sea
filled with the slow, sure breath of sleeping cattle,
the hiss and clutter of their stirring
and a horizon that doesn't pitch and waver.

I'm self-gaffed dragging avid death behind me
closed inside this narrow wooden stage,
without soil or bloom or leaf or riparian glitter.
Years have stained me, soot-scribed by the same boiling flames
that redden the hell-stinking smoke's black belly and the pendant clouds.
Over and over, whip-slung back to sea,
drawn by that voiceless great grave fish
and the thought of his death
that drives me from your safe haven
calms the sharp chop of my mind
like God's fragrant oil anointing Jonah's storm
gentling the sea to long slow swells.
Chasing leviathan—bond and covenant
to ruined, God-flimflammed Job.

Chapter 68

Deborah Meadows
   from *The Theory of Subjectivity in* Moby-Dick

Skin remains a question:
"what and where is the skin of the whale?"

What and where is the mind?
      Inscribed upon, see through
      a brittle clarity, read through spectacles
that make a skin
over skin.

Upon the printed page or
      written into flesh as
warm-blooded as "we"
yet indecipherable.

Quarters for a child
      assuming one more tender
      than skin—
bulk mysterious, yet
      phenomena present how
      rocks connect
      to pyramids, as made things.

Borneo
man of nature, specimen body
with skin parsed for warmth.
Specimen-skin made, marked, for sale.

Comfortable with risk, copied
      to dominant collection of twoness
dispersed by instruments
      identical
to how small easy pieces
can be rendered
and teach these fine creatures how.

Chapter 69

Deborah Meadows
    from *The Theory of Subjectivity in* Moby-Dick

I am nearly lost in this panorama.

Still colossal except the insatiate surface
    on which plays whale reduction.

        Mock funeral screams
lie where flesh represents
waste, where illustration-told
opens space onto fiction.

Further from the ship, the ghost whale
    creates "presence," its representation
    floats in the mind for years,
so shun the place, and in so doing
    make tradition, mark orthodoxy.
Geographic "sheep leap over a vacuum"
    that lies where the reduced poem
    represents excess, where illustration-told
forecloses place onto strange love.

Chapter 92: Ambergris

Jessica Cuello

His desire pins a strange eye,
takes measure of my inside.
I am oblivious to this resin,
to this mine—a perfume

hardened in my bowels,
to take when I am dead, to take
secretions of the throat.
My guts are lined with spine and beak.

Labor makes it sweet.
I can't see the whole he sees.
He's seen the veins, the skin, the grey.

Does he grope for this rock
that I carry like an organ—
an afterthought—that I do not even carry.

Ambergris

Lee Upton

"What then shall I liken the sperm whale to for fragrance, considering his magnitude?
Must it not be to that famous elephant, with jewelled tusks, and redolent with myrrh,
which was led out of an Indian town to do honour to Alexander the Great?"
  Moby-Dick, Chapter 92: "Ambergris"

What was expelled from the vast body, bobbed for decades,
    turned silvery, then was netted, and sailed to France?
In the hanging gardens of a shop,
    pollen brushes against eyelashes,
and a current of scent spins in a draft,
    while outside the perfumer's window
willows drip, and cedars glisten
    in the sunlight's chemistry.
Inside, here, water droplets rise like clear blood
    on the pleats of petals,
and moths drift over a beaker,
    and a bit of ambergris melts to the size of a raindrop.
A slight sweet musty odor
    steams up. Paradise sinks a root
in a barnyard.
    So much can be made of the whale—
that muse with a burnished blowhole,
    with inky squid-bottling guts,
with an entry port tougher than any writer's nibs, and
    with unending intestines: the noble point of origin, from which
arises a waxen husk to float,
    to be sought as a crusted mystery,
not another jewel
    so much as a seam of deep night soil,
opened, lucrative, freed from a being
    whose brain weighed,
we may estimate,
    near five times
that of Alexander the Great's—
    ambergris—
to dab right there
    behind a small human ear.

Articulation

Nicholas Spengler

"Sir Clifford's whale has been articulated throughout; so that, like a great chest of drawers, you can open and shut him, in all his bony cavities . . . "
   Moby-Dick, Chapter 102: "A Bower in the Arsacides"

I. Definition

The linking of sounds
meaningless alone
into speech—or bones

Into a trellis for body
and breath, the joint
on which we all hinge;

But also: a system
for making things discrete,
so many scores on a sheet—

The marks by which we measure
creation, catalogue
its constituent parts,

Folio and *Octavo*,
ways to fold and divide
like drawers we slide

Open, to find a lamp,
an ampulla of holy oil,
a jar of lightning—

Anything to illuminate
and preserve us from
the ungraspable phantom.

II. Application

First, in sea or in earth
submerge the remains
until flesh falls away

Then wash the bones
in peroxide, let them dry
in the sun, number them

With a grease pencil
and arrange them on a bare floor
like so many scores

So you can picture the whole—
not just the skeleton
suspended, a ghost in the hall,

But how the living thing moves
flukes unfurled
at the limit of two worlds

Needing one as much as the other:
now sounding the depths,
now breaching for breath—

As the cry goes out aloft
and labors of blood and lungs increase
to hunt the uncanny half-known beast.

III. Apology
(Ishmael to Queequeg)

I dreamed I was an island
insular and alone,
lost in latitudes unknown—

Or a whale in the arctic,
warm-blooded citadel
in an empire of ice;

But I awoke in your arms
snug—a spark
in winter's hyperborean heart

And I felt myself melt in you:
we made a fire
wherein the bond was forged,

Antipodal souls now jointed
like a hinge, and we joined the crew
a joint-stock company of two.

Except I alone survived the wreck
buoyed and orphaned by death
as your princely body sank—

May your bones be a bower
for the ocean's glowing life, a barricade
against this cannibal world we've made.

Ishmael Na My Name

Onyinye Miriam Uwolloh

[From Chapters 1-12]

Ishmael na my name
My heart dey do me somehow
I dey go whaling
Coin no dey my purse
As cold dey catch me so tey
I go Spouter Inn
Dey give me roommate
Na so he come be savage
He come fear me o
As I come wake up
His hand come dey for blanket
Na so we be friends

We dey waka go
And admire New Bedford
Whaling be im life
Queequeg na pagan
But im get a good heart sha
Na padi be that
I dey comfortable
His smoke no dey disturb me
He begin dey talk
Na Kokovoko
Na im be Queequeg home town
Na so he tell me

[From Chapters 13-24]

Na from Nantucket
Wey dey very small for map
Good whalers dey come
Peleg dey vex me
He no wan hire Queequeg
Skill beat religion
Prophet come yarn us
I think say im be mad man
We come ignore am

Ship go soon leave port
Aunty Charity dey fuss
Ahab never show
We come see shadows
Elijah come yarn again
Captain still no show
Whaling get im pride
Yale and Harvard na my schools
Honor dey this work

[From Chapters 25-36]

Chief mate na Starbuck
Him be good Nantucket man
Courage dey im heart
Stubb and Flask follow
Queequeg, Daggoo, Tashtego
Na dem dey hunt whales
One day I come see
Ahab on top Pequod deck
One leg dey missing
Him temper dey hot
Na so im dey shout at Stubb
Stubb no like am oo

Ahab come dey smoke
He come throw pipe for ocean
Which kain man be dis?
Cetology sha
I go use am classify
Plenty plenty whales
When you dey mast-head
If you no pay attention
Na so you go fall
For seeing white whale
The reward na one doubloon
Ahab talk am so

[From Chapters 37-48]

Starbuck no get peace
Im know say Ahab no well
Him fit do nothing
The sailors dey dance
The party dey make sense but
Fight and wind spoil am
The white whale story
Na so dem dey tell me so
No one fit catch am
Why white get power?
Why it dey fear men sometimes?
Moby Dick dey white

For night noise dey sound
But we no see who talk am
Na bad food cause am?
Ahab dey obsessed
Him dey use tools and his men
White whale no show face
I come dey weave mat
Na so e resemble Fate
Tashtego sight whale
I dey for the boat
The whale come destroy am oo
We come dey water

[From Chapters 49-60]

As dem rescue us
Na so I come write my will
That na my fourth time
Moby Dick chop Radney
Steelkit come dey happy oo
Na Town-Ho story

Ahab get im men
Na dem be the noisy ghosts
Crew fear Fedallah
Na so something rise
Daggoo talk say na white whale
But im be white squid

[From Chapters 61-72]

Pequod come sight whale
Water dey churn, blood dey spill
Na Stubb wey kill am
Stubb dey bully Fleece
As he wan chop whale steak fast
Fleece come preach instead

Whale dey hang for ship
Na so shark come dey chop am
Dem fit chop humans
But the head remain
Ahab come ask am questions
The head no fit talk

[From Chapters 73-84]

Tashtego come slip
Him and head come dey sink but
Queequeg rescue am
Whale no get a nose
But im head get dignity
You fit read the brow?

We come meet the Virgin
Dem dey race us for whale oil
Our old whale come sink
Whaling get glory
Pictures and legends show am
Club members dey great

[From Chapters 85-96]

Since before before
Whales just dey spout for ocean
Na so dem dey breathe
E also be like
All things wey dey for world be
Fast-fish and loose-fish

Pequod meet Rosebud
Stubb come use cunny cunny
Collect Ambergris
Pip dey jump from boat
Stubb warm am, e come leave am
Ocean turn im mad

[From Chapters 97-108]

As Doubloon dey deck
Crew dey look am one by one
Dem see different things
Captain Boomer come
Since e lose im arm to whale
Im try warn Ahab

Na for Arascides
I measure whale skeleton
Tattoo dey right arm
Ahab come break leg
As e come pierce im before
Im call carpenter

[From Chapters 109-120]

Starbuck come talk but
Ahab point gun for im head
Starbuck leave cabin
As Queequeg come sick
Im ask for coffin but he
Come recover well
As im dey the forge
Na so Ahab bring harpoon
And baff am for blood

Pequod come sight whales
Crew come catch four, but Ahab
Still dey feel im gloom
Na so Typhoon come
Fear come catch all crew members
But Ahab no gree
Starbuck try yarn him
About the Pequod damage
But e no listen

[From Chapters 121-132]

Tashtego dey mast
"I no like this thunder oo"
Na so im dey talk
Starbuck come pick the
Gun Ahab point for im but
E no fit kill im
Na so carpenter
Come turn Queequeg coffin to
Life buoy for Pequod
Ahab come notice
Na coffin wey go save lives

E go yarn with Pip
The Rachel come say
Make Pequod help dem find boy
Ahab heart dey cold
Pip follow Ahab
But Captain no wan hear im
Pip still dey yarn sha
Ahab mood dey black
Im obsession dey increase
Hawk come steal im hat
Upon all im lose

60

[Chapters 133-Epilogue]

Upon all Starbuck come talk
Ahab no fit stop
Moby Dick come show
Na Ahab wey sight am oo
Im own boat no wreck
On top second day
The whale come break Ahab leg
Fedallah come die
Ahab shout at whale
E come drown for harpoon rope
Ship sink, crew perish
Only me wey live
I come dey float for coffin
Rachel rescue me

Ishmael's PTSD

Elizabeth Schultz

He clasped the coffin as it churned
in the creaming maelstrom, curving
around insensible oars and spars,

until he floated free onto the ocean's
immense and indecipherable softness.
His saviors wrapped him in a hammock,

the survivor, the young son returned
to them, seeking to bandage
his soul's gashes. Adrift in stupor,

he heard the men's voices from all
the sea's isles, whispering to him
like waves, chastising his heart's coast.

Who knows if he slept, dreaming
of that rumpled bed in New Bedford
or of the ship's mesmerizing fire?

Who knows if the whale's thud continued
to resonate through his splintered timbers,
or if, seeing God's foot upon the treadle

of the loom, he began to speak in tongues?
In mid-ocean, he could post no broadsides,
order no black-bordered, marble tablets.

It's known that coming home, the shore
burned his soles, that he headed
for the Poles, Patagonia, Peru,

Africa, Turkey, Paris, Cologne,
circumnavigating back to the Catskills
and inland waters. En route, he swam

through libraries, museums, cathedrals,
and tattooed himself with notes
in remembrance of his bosom friend

and of the whales they'd scratched,
and so began his own mystical treatise.
Meeting him, they said he's haunted,

that he'd fixed his fiery sights
on mightier, stranger foes than whales.
Little could they fathom his losses

to the swirling maelstrom
and the ocean's open blankness.
He sailed once more into the Pacific,

soothed by its ebb and flow against
continents, its unceasing cradling
of drowned dreams and souls. In time,

reaching the Arsacides, he witnessed,
with equal eye, the weaving of life's
green tendrils with death's white bones,

and at last, grasping the ungraspable,
he wrote it.

Enveloped in Whale Lines

Michalle Gould

here is a rifled heart, half-unhinged,
by the visible absence of the whale;
bare words and facts cannot sustain
his vision of that beast, twice risen
to the surface; he needs the very thing
before him; as a relic or an omen,
its being is no more than an almighty
forlornness, an outline and skeleton
lacking flesh and muscle, mere lath
and plaster, where he desires a wall.
This mortar will not clamp to the surface,
it has no stick to it. Therefore, what
is he left with? Only a pile of dust
and a scrimp of gray skin: one day
they will say that such a creature
never really could have existed

Re-Incarnating *Moby-Dick*

Prelude

Ivan Klein

Herman Melville
I walk in your shoes
around Manhattos,

In your poor coat I feel
the November chill / at water's edge
wonder dumb at the God of heaven.

I make my peace with savages,
forget Christian hospitality
& look for a ship (to sail the world)
to find the beast that eats me up.

Frankincense

Mira Dougherty-Johnson

Etymology

frank·in·cense
ˈfraNGkənˌsens/
noun: **frankincense**
1. an aromatic gum resin obtained from an African tree and burned as incense
   Webster's Dictionary Online

Lexicon Entry: λίβᾰνος [ῐ], ὁ, *frankincense-tree, Boswellia Carterii,* Hdt.4.75, Thphr.*HP*9.4.2, Dsc.1.68, etc.; ἱερόδακρυς λ. Melanipp.I.5. II.= λιβανωτός, *frankincense* in which sense it is feminine in Pi.Fr.I 22.3, E.Ba.I 44 (lyr.); but masculine in *PCair.Zen.*69.13 iii B.C., *AP*6.231 (Phil.), 9.93 (Antip. Thess.), *Edict. Diocl.* ('Αθηνα 18.6, Tegea); indeterminate in Sapph. *Supp.*20C.2, *S.Fr.*1064, Anaxandr.41.37, *SIG* 247ii 19 (Delph., iv B.C.). [4]
Frankincense, subs. Ar. and P. λῐβᾰνωτός (ed. *libanotos*), ὁ. Incense for burning: P. and V. θῡμιᾱμᾰτα (ed. *thumiamata* - incense), τά.
The origin of the word is uncertain.
"Before 1398 fraunkencense, in Trevisa's translation of Bartholomew's *De Proprietatibus* Rerum; apparently from Old French *frank* genuine or true, and *encens* incense."
Frank comes from the Latin *Francus, of or belonging to the Franks.* Incense comes from the Latin *incensum, a setting fire to, lighting, incense.*
Another explanation sees the word as a combination of the Old French word *franc* meaning "pure" or "abundant," added to the Latin word *incensum,* meaning "to kindle." Still others say that it means "the incense of the Franks," because during the Crusades, the Franks re-introduced it to Europe.

— Hellenismos Dictionary Online

Extracts

And when they were come into the house, they saw the young child with Mary his mother, and fell down, and worshipped him: and when they had opened their treasures, they presented unto him gifts; gold, and frankincense, and myrrh. – The Bible

Many the lumps of frankincense on the same altar; one falls there early and another late, but it makes no difference. – Marcus Aurelius

Though fame is smoke, its fumes are frankincense to human thoughts. – Lord Byron

The words which express our faith and piety are not definite yet they are significant and fragrant like frankincense to superior natures. – Henry David Thoreau

You are all camphire and frankincense, all chastity and odour. – William Congreve

I don't know when pepper mills in a restaurant got to be right behind frankincense and myrrh in prominence. It used to be in a little jar that sat next to the salt on the table and everyone passed it around, sneezed, and it was no big deal. – Erma Bombeck

Who is this that cometh out of the wilderness like pillars of smoke, perfumed with myrrh and frankincense, with all powders of the merchant? Behold his bed, which is Solomon's; threescore valiant men are about it, of the valiant of Israel. – The Bible

And the LORD said unto Moses, Take unto thee sweet spices, stacte,
and onycha,and galbanum; these sweet spices with pure frankincense:
of each shall there be a like weight:
And thou shalt make it a perfume, a confection after
the art of the apothecary, tempered together, pure and holy:
And thou shalt beat some of it very small, and put of it before
the testimony in the tabernacle of the congregation,
where I will meet with thee: it shall be unto you most holy. – The Bible

Lives there the man with soul so dead as to disown the wish
to merit the people's applause, and having uttered words worthy
to be kept in cedar oil to latest times, to leave behind him
rhymes that dread neither herrings nor frankincense. – Persius

And if there come the singers, and the dancers and the flute players—buy of their gifts also. For they too are gatherers of fruit and frankincense, and that which they bring, though fashioned of dreams, is raiment and food for your soul. – Khalil Gibran

Chapter 1

Flarings

Call me Eurydice.[1] Some years ago—ten, as many fingers as I have to hold— my father, having lost his wife, my spectral mother, to a damp chill in the air, and, thus, his partnership in the trades alongside his bereft father-in-law, had a thought to travel the dusty camel roads for a while and see the desert lands of the world. It is a way he has of fending off the clinking empty bottles, the sweet dark tar of his glass pipe. Whenever he finds himself staring down the hollow, feeling the arid Harmattan[2] gust through the concavity of his soul; whenever he finds himself kicking up small piles of sand in the alley near the liquor store, or falling asleep on the bench in the main square blazed by the sun; and especially when his compulsions spill into his spleen, when his ire gets the best of him, when he looks into my face, which is my ghostly mother's face, and tries to stop himself a pinch or punch— that is when we must to Africa. This is his standby, his fallback for detox, rehab, the thick white casing of a straightjacket. Like Rilke penned sonnets from his Swiss sanatorium and Pound composed cantos in St. Elizabeth's, my father sets his sights on Danakil.[3] I am not surprised by this. All men, if they knew it in their hearts, cherish this kind of extreme, share a craving for emboldened survival in a doomed, bone-scattered wasteland.

There is your Gulf of Aden,[4] clear and warm, stabbed through by the keels and hulls of boats, toothed masts pricking the bleached counterpane of the sky. There is your vast Indian Ocean, the waves curling like pale kittens along the shore, their leavings the small scraps of fouled foam. But look! Here is where my father brought me, the Afar Triangle,[5] cracked swathes of pasty salt flats, a parched boomerang of dirt-colored land. Here is where we make our new hearth, a patch of scraggled Boswellia trees, a canvas tent, a sky of stars to sleep under, an unrelenting wind. There is magic in it. There is magic in the sap of the trees we cut. Magic in how the bubbling resin heals, how it in turn has its own secret cures. There is magic in the camel my father swapped his watch for, its watery eye and sacred internal reservoir. There is a way we remake ourselves every day, going about in our long muslin trousers, the scarves we drape about our heads, the shush and cluck our tongues make when we are in the souk,[6] the practiced way our hands fold the softened American dollars, the way our eyes turn down but our dress-up crosses flash—a coruscation in the air—when we exchange news with the cossetted merchants of the cloth. Have you seen them? Their corpulence, their flatulence trapped in the weave of their coarse brown robes? Their carbuncles, deltas of blood vessels straining their flaccid cheeks? Walking amongst those who have gone hungry? Breathing into their cupped embroidered handkerchiefs? I name no names. But shame upon them! Hold one fist high, raised toward the sky. Shame upon all cowards—Hist! I hear leather beyond! My father hangs his camel tack. His heavy breath follows not far behind.

Notes

1. In Greek mythology, Eurydice was an oak nymph and one of the daughters of Apollo. She was the wife of Orpheus, who tried to bring her back from the dead with his enchanting music.

2. Dry northerly wind across central Africa

3. Desert area on the Somali peninsula

4. A gulf located in the Arabian Sea between Yemen, on the south coast of the Arabian Peninsula, and Somalia in the Horn of Africa

5. One of the hottest places year-round anywhere on Earth (77 °F to 118 °F); also well known as one of the cradles of extinct hominins

6. An open-air marketplace or commercial quarter in Middle Eastern and North African cities

Moby-Dick for Modern Readers

Waldo Gemio

Call me.
Or email.
We'll meet at Starbuck's.
Have a whale of a time.
And speak of the legend of Mocha Dick
the real name of Melville's inspiration for Moby
or you could read your mobi-book

You can bring your flask
if you keep it hidden
like the meaning of the book
unless you think it's about manifest destiny
or the nature of white
or the nature of black
or a homo-erotic fantasy
or racism in America
(manifest destiny again)

Ishmael sounds like a drunk slurring his post
picking up his post
Ishmael
Ish another fucking bill

And if we're lucky
like Ishmael
we'll survive the others
as well as ourselves

Big Comeback Tour

Bob McGowan

Here comes Moby Dick
heading up the Mississippi
from the delta

past poisoned mussel beds
ghosts of freshwater pearls
tumorous sturgeon

great sperm bent
on sirin' liberty
conceive a new nation

flat forehead wrinkled
like a flag
pushing parabolic crest

turning heartland inside
out like a ball
new womb altogether

flukes roil cleanse
sand bars batter bridges
overwhelming dikes

sounds like a grand guignole
tragedy moves upstream
revenge on kids and all

cows balloon by
snag on corn crib
scene by Bosch

ol' Huck an' Jim
stick out thumbs
to slow him down

he swallows 'em up
among his ribs they
greet their personal Gepetto

here's the truth
big whitey upchucks 'em
on the levee

prophets of the flood plain
proclaim new Jerusalemic
suburbs of Atlantis

share their dream
few victims understand
but somebody's going to get it

As My Uncle Rides an Exercise Bike at the Rec Center, He Tries to Explain *Moby-Dick* to the Man Riding Beside Him

John Struloeff

Moby Dick. Moby . . . *Dick*. Hear that?
It just sounds funny.
I wonder if your average American
in 1851 knew what "dick" really means.
And "moby"? Sounds like bloaty, or booby.
Don't know what the hell that's supposed to mean.
And it's just a damn dirty tale when you get down
to it. It all starts with Ishmael—
Ich, which is German for "I"
and "mael," *male*, as in, "I am male"—
getting into bed with a tattooed man,
and I've never heard of a story,
up to any good, that started
with a man getting into bed with another man
with tattoos all up and down his arms.
Then they get on this tiny little boat,
just a bunch of lonely men, on the *Pequod*,
little humping peas in a pod,
sailing the high seas, and before long
their captain swaggers his way to deck,
wearing some frilly outfit
and he's got a big hard peg leg,
which the whole crew's staring at.
Now, everybody knows that peg leg
stands for "erection" in dirty people's talk.

And of course, this guy's running the show.
No surprise, he informs them loud and clear,
that this boat is after some sperm whales,
and there just happens to be one special
white whale out there that looks like one big sperm.
This whale happens to be named Dick,
and Dick and Cap'n Ahab share some harsh feelings,
namely a Moses-like wrathful revenge
they would like to sling at each other,
stemming from some mysterious rendezvous
they shared in their distant nautical pasts.
In other words, a jealous brawl's about to take place.
Now, these fellas search high and low,
with Cap'n Ahab at the wheel, humping along,
yelling every five minutes, "Thar she blows!"
and low and behold, another one blows,
until that fateful day when Ahab sees his Dick again.
God Almighty, it's one hell of a fight.
A whole crew full of men trying to wrestle
this Dick down, until Ahab lets her fly
and Ahab, Dick, and crew are swallowed up,
descending into blissful oblivion, all holding each other.
Now, what I don't understand, is why
Ishmael is left floating on a coffin
in the middle of the deep blue sea.

Loomings

Elizabeth Schultz

I've read the book so often
its phrases pave my speech
and pierce my dreams. It
made clear that men can be
demons, and whales miracles.

And I've sailed several seas
and spotted whales enough
to fill a cetologist's log.
I've learned that respect
is what I owe old Ocean.

Yet, for nights before
the *Morgan* sailed, I slept
with knotted hands and restless
feet, paced a deck crowded
with ungraspable phantoms.

I had visions of the ship,
swathed, wreathed in mists,
fog horns bleating, a whited
sepulcher. I lost faith in its
solid futtocks of black locust.

At noon I heard an old friend's
big laughter in a sushi shack.
But he'd become a shrunken
vestige of himself, reminding
me of responsibilities ashore.

I vomited up my lobster roll,
but convinced I was fated for this
voyage, hoisted my carpet bag,
prepared to meet my mates from
all the earth's occupations.

At last, on the *Morgan's* wide
deck, and dazzled, I stumbled
over a skylight and knocked
my head on a hatch. But clicking
off my cell phone, I let the masts
point me heavenward, and
the wonder-world sprang open.

Oil that Lights the World

Elizabeth Schultz

Sailing off the grid,
the *Pequod* and the old
Morgan kept themselves
well-lit. Barrels of crude
filled their hulls. Tracing
over his charts in search
of one whale, Ahab could
well afford to burn
the midnight oil, while
the *Morgan's* masters
struck it rich for decades,
blessed with greasy luck.

Larger, harsher harpoons,
electrified to run all night,
still plunder the deep heart
of earth and sea to light
the world, and so now
as the dark *Morgan* lies
at anchor, drenched in
moonlight, her motherboard
winks in astral patterns
of red, blue, and green.
Lights switch on, off in
a high-tech web of safety,
comfort, friends, all that's
kind to our mortalities.

On Deck

Elizabeth Schultz

No one notices the relics
of slaughter, fluke posts,
hawser holes, the cutting
stage where Leviathan
was hung from the side
and hoisted up in pieces,
where flesh was severed
from the bones, where
whale steak might be had
for dinner. The fiery try-
works, where blubber was
rendered into the oil that
ran empires, are overlooked
as obsolete antiques or
photographed for analysis.
On deck, no longer awash
in gore and entrails, men,
once engaged in a bloody
butchery of a business, now
ponder the whole ocean's
salvation.

The *Morgan* On Stellwagen Bank

Elizabeth Schultz

We sailed amidst them,
out on Stellwagen Bank,
the old ship, no longer
armed with barbs or tricked
out with lances, but newly
rigged, spreading fresh
canvas on all masts, rising
up, up, upon the waves,
joyous and reborn and soaring.

We met them on their
playground, a minke first,
arched and glistening,
forerunner for the humpbacks,
who frolicked in a pod,
splashing, somersaulting,
making waves, their fins,
long white angels' wings,
gyrating, beating upward
out of the sea, before diving
down, down, their signature
tails following them, curved
and hovering, heart-shaped,
shining, before dissolving
into depths, the flukes now
phantasmagoric shadows,
leaving shearwaters and terns,
circling like visible echoes
above their churning,

while we leaned out
on the ship's rail, intent
on a second coming,
awed by such exuberance,
yearning for forgiveness.

Lifting the Shroud

Elizabeth Schultz

It was a mild, mild day,
a convergence of forms,
of movement, of sound,
beyond narrative, beyond linearity,
the *Morgan* arriving, her sails,
layered wings unfolding, opening,
a flock of white birds, pivoting
together on her masts, humpbacks'
fins rotating, swirling white
banners, up from azure depths,
whales suffusing, blowing off
steam, a whale boat rowing
in harmony, out from the ship,
the boat steerer calling, reach,
catch, and pull, oars sweeping
together, a chorus line, tapping
the backs of whales, whales
rubbing the boats' keels, bubble-
netting, people applauding, terns
and shearwaters, pirouetting,
ruffling the air, flashes of foam,
alighting, riding waves, white
clouds, white sails surging
and swelling over blue waters,
all simultaneous, all synchronized,
dancing, lifting the great shroud
of the sea.

Melville in the Enchanted Nursery

Laurie Robertson-Lorant

One mild Pacific day as we were cruising
past the low-shaded coves and islands of Sumatra,
where spice ships ply their trade on the China Sea,
I saw on the horizon rings of mist
sparkling and pluming in the noonday air,
fountains of silver spray.

We hit a lone bull, who dragged us, then broke free,
hurtling our boat between two basking whales
into a lagoon where I could see
suspended in watery vaults, a pod of whales,
great nursing mothers with their suckling calves.
My shipmates, harpoons dangling, stood transfixed
watching the baby whales draw from the milk
a spiritual sustenance as they gazed skyward.

The grand armada floats, and I float with them
as, buoyed by my body and cradled by one fluke,
my newborn tugs my breast and gulps his food,
cord slack between us, his eyes like pearly pools.

I am mother of milkiness, dalliance and delight.
Flanks brushing continents, I circumnavigate the globe
breaching whenever I feel the urge to fly,
shouting "Mammal, Mammal, Mammal!" at the sky.

Whale Watching

Anthony Caleshu

Ever since you were born, I have been re-reading;
I am blinded by excessive marks of punctuation.
I use them in order to pause where I like: in the supermarket
in front of the cereals or two-for-one prawns;
on the dual carriage way on the way to Dartington
to walk you under the river oaks. Yesterday, it was February
and when we pulled back the curtains
we saw it was still dark and our car was still shining
under the sodium street lamp and the neighborhood watch sticker.
I could tell you were wondering whose car you were in,
and whose room I was in, whose house we two were in,
shuffling between floors, from bedroom to kitchen,
stepping in and out of sleep, as if in and out of seasons.
I don't have to tell you that it has been a long Winter.
I promise you this: when we go to sea we will wear hats
and stand starboard as sailors. We will ride waves
and watch for whales sounding on the horizon,
silent as our thoughts. Those of us who are awake and above water
have little right to have salt blown in our faces, but we feel it nonetheless.
Already it is May. I rock you in my arms like a comma.

Pip

Adam Day

for Eric Garner

Guy behind me
asks his friend,

"Why're black boys
so loud

in the middle
of movies."

Because privilege
is silent. The silver

screen whale
sets off

a dark water
figure

beneath night.
Neither can be

killed. They're
already dead.

The Drowning

Jeff Saperstein

So my mind went back to Alabama
and that swimming pond Daddy taught me
to paddle in before they sold him away.
You couldn't ever be far from shore
and there was Daddy to grab onto
or the dangling limbs of those cottonwoods.
Now, when the last boat slipped away,
there was nothing to reach for in this immensity.
I hadn't asked to ship an oar but Mr. Stubb said
I didn't read the fine print
so there I was in the bows, next to wild Tashtego,
who had fire in his eyes, and I felt it again,
that phantom kick at the keel which Stubb said
was just a playful tap of the flukes.

Now it was dark and the sky filled with icy stars.
My fingers went numb, my arms grew heavy
and then I was under, my ears filling
with the cries of orphan seals, plummeting
past the bloated corpses of slaves
thrown overboard to lighten the load
in a storm, passing coral insects,
jelly fish and giant squid, eyeless creatures
from the days before God made men.
And sinking deeper, lit by the lurid light,
there was Daddy, caught in the convoluted coils
of the line, fast fish to the big white fish
whose lidless eye held no pity.

The Ambiguities

Jeff Saperstein

The Whale is the World:
    the ultimate Other;
    your tattooed Brother;
    that omnipotent Mother
with a dick the size of New York.

The Whiteness of the Whale

Jim LaVilla-Havelin

is not the whiteness of the cattle egret
    slipping through the white hot Texas sky
    over heavy cows

and not Diego's calla lilies, cups overflowing with
    the worth of the world

the whiteness of the whale is not the whiteness of the rain lilies,
    slight and timely and gone

substantial, the whiteness of the whale
    of weddings in the west and funerals in the east

    chalk

    clouds

    porcelain

    the fades in PERSONA and SHAME

snow, from the heart of our memory

    purity
    no collage

memory
no redemption

    obsession and no resolution

memory from the heart of

    for twenty years I'd write
    a whale poem for Eleanor

    now, mother, gone, and a mother herself,
    her Tessa stands on a beach on a coast
    in a whole different century

    the whiteness of the whale
    is the long corridor into now

and now
confronted by the blank page
enormous, white
    a snowy field, a terror, an emptiness

the peril, the challenge
    to improve upon
    the blank page, the whiteness

    eggs

    soap

    refrigerators, stoves

is not the whiteness of the cattle egret
    fleeting, folding, flying
    graceful across the sky

or the Parthenon
white timeless
        after the paint peeled

    is the whiteness
        of Ryman and Simic and Pahmuk,

    pearls

    and
    larger than literature
    even than life

rising out of white sea foam, white
white and mountainous
white and memorable
and wondrous and hopeful and terrible
       white

xi.)

Diane Raptosh

Zygote,
  Lucky for you: You can't pick up
that robocall's race-cry-out limnic eruption ~~ #$^@*!?*^.

Shit happens as Whiteness
  shovels around

   on its   peg leg
      whump

This means I might have to teach you
key habits of Melville's whole novel

by borrowing
algebra's alphabet.
Through using some logic equations:

A. Forms of propositions.

   a. Moby Dick is a whale.
   b. A whale is a mammal.
   c. Moby Dick is Ahab's enemy.
   d. Moby Dick is not the devil.

   e. Ishmael is not albino.
   f. Ishmael is Moby Dick's friend.
   g. Ishmael is not God.
   h. Moby Dick is not a fish.

   i. Moby Dick defeats Ahab.
   j. Ahab is meaner than the devil.
   k. Ishmael is everyone's friend.
   l. Ahab is not Ishmael's enemy.

   m. Moby Dick is albino.
   n. No one is meaner than Ahab.
   o. Ahab is meaner than anyone.
   p. God is not a whale.

   q. The devil is no one's friend.
   r. Ahab has no friends.
   s. Ishmael does not defeat Ahab.
   t. God is not the devil.

B. Exceptives and superlatives.

a. Everyone except Ahab fears Moby Dick. $(Zxy \equiv x \text{ fears } y)$
b. No one except Ahab can defeat Moby Dick.
c. Moby Dick is the only albino whale.

d. Only Ishmael is a friend of Moby Dick.

e. No one is meaner than Ahab except the devil.
f. Every whale except Moby Dick is a friend of Ahab.
g. There are other whales besides Moby Dick that are feared by Ishmael.

Helpful abbreviations.

a = Ahab; d = the devil; g = God; I = Ishmael; m = Moby Dick; $Ax \equiv x \text{ is albino}$; $Fx \equiv x \text{ is a fish}$; $Mx \equiv x \text{ is a mammal}$; $Px \equiv x \text{ is a person}$; $Wx \equiv x \text{ is a whale}$; $Dxy \equiv x \text{ defeats } y$; $Exy \equiv x \text{ is an enemy of } y$; $Fxy = \equiv \text{ is a friend of } y$; $Mxy \equiv x \text{ is meaner than } y$; $Sxy \equiv x \text{ is swifter than } y$.

So then. I = Ishmael. Oh might as well,
since x is a mammal,
and they're pretty quick. Besides which,

as soon as I slip
into cypher's forecastle
I'm free. You cannot undo

the done-unto-you,
but you can forgive it. Tonight I'm feeling like
forming ex-expletives,

something like apeshit's
shapeshift to lippy-glug happiness.
Zygote, you'll get it:

every egg has an X,
every leg wants a dress,
Moby Dick is no devil,

which means every Ahab
must locate beings
on whom they can offload the whale

of their innermost torment:
May be the one grave
disease of our day. I = Ishmael.

Px ≡ x is a person.
A person.
Life Speck, by now, maybe

you're newly sized
to a raw sesame seed.
Already you are

what World will call *girl*
or a *guy*, but here's the P.S.:
Female = the default sex,

probably precisely
because *x is swifter than y,*
where here we let *swift* mean *gifted*

in souped-up stillness. Why is it
Zxy ≡ x fears y? Sometimes y really
starts to stick it to x and somehow

that's supposed to be *Sxy.* Maybe y will get
a chance to leaven himself. . . . Sometimes
Moby is just a vegan musician, whereas,

Zygote, I think you more or less
fish-person, or *FxPx.* Hang on to the winch
of all this shape-shifting!

Being able to sidle the glide of another
is what preserves us. And who would deny
that Biblical Ishmael doubled

as more or less donkey-mankind
or that Melville's narrator-self is *spec*
consciousness? Sentences are

sentience's avatars:
They are Negative Capability's
Citizens' United,

but alas this plows us into new ships
far at sea. *d = the devil.*
And cruelty's *Mxy.* Both

of them gather as I not quite
whistle *Ishmael*-Dixie and maybe
twelve nieces shall I beget,

90

who will multiply
all that sits opposite meanness exceedingly,
at the same time as they become

badass in archery. Goddishness
is not a whale, isn't something
given to *is*-ing or not, so let us declare-ask

a quotient: *The first
1,000-year-old person's
already been born?*

Zygote, Life Speck,
oh, just say
Everyone: Let's get un-*Exy*.

We're wearing identical tentacles,
and I know I am mapping out days
of my nights through the specs

of my ending-most seconds
even though I'm not there yet. This is the way
to place-date me in spacetime, there

with the barely conceived—that Fertilize-Nation
through whose fallopian truths all manner of thing
gains fragility's strength.

There's nothing
that couldn't not happen,
world without end

rigging its fishy iFriends,
its run-away jibs,
and yes, sometimes loving

is mouthy and awful
but there's no other force
earnest enough in a world this peckish

in which x might end up fishibian,
in which x is a mammal
in which x is a kiss

whose finity gushes exchange
of 80-plus million ginned up bacteria,
noble for their binary fission, their frenemy swiftness.

"In a few minutes, however, he was missed by his shipmates, and being, it seems, for some reason a huge favorite with them, they raised a cry of 'Bulkington! Bulkington! Where's Bulkington?' and darted out of the house in pursuit of him."

Louis Phillips

Where shall we look
For this man called Bulkington?
Try the eye-stalk of good deeds,
Mount the ferris wheel of dust,
Spit under the lugsail.
We once sat him on the Stone of Sconce
& crowned him the Wharf Rat King.

Where shall we look?
Hurry the trysail into place,
& tax the water's spout
Luff his image into a tankard.
Conjure him, voodoo him,
Swivel the Book of the Dead.
Was he keel-hauled
Thru witches' brew?

Someone is missing.
Someone is no longer here.

"But here is an artist. He desires to paint you the dreamiest, shadiest, quietest, most enchanting bit of romantic landscape in all the valley of the Saco. What is the chief element he employs?"

Louis Phillips

There in the sycamore
Wind without wrinkle—mere
Leaf trace where

Nicked by shadows hither,
Amid road warblers & heather,
Toadflax smothers

The hummock edgeways,
Narrowed quiet sways
Ever so slightly, glazed

By air's humid daub, flirt
At a fragrant edge, sport
Of nightjars over moneywort.

The moon is lodged so fierce,
It too must rise. Terse
& jagged, all things thirst.

"All visible objects, man, are but as pasteboard masks."

Louis Phillips

& wore the mask of the world too tight
Thru which he saw nothing he could strike
A bargain with. The Real was sudden
With its heavy freight, when into his light
Sharked a sandskin world. The day was stark.
There are those who can make a life
From anything. Ideas, sang Plato from his cave,
Ideas alone are real. I am but a sodden

Shadow, tho that shadow take a wife.
My hand's a mask & my mouth, he laughed.
But still he practiced how to snare
Portions for his touch. We test the air
With pralltrilled music, thru & thru.
Disdain this pranking world? Go to. Go to.

"Why then do you try to 'enlarge' your mind? Subtilize it."

Louis Phillips

There are terrible events to consider,
Grand & obscene.
On 42nd Street,
One black whore has been beat,
& her white pimp
Has cleared out.
You know the rest,
Tho the rest is none too neat

A traffic light blinks
Red & green.
The cops arrive 10 minutes late.
Under a yellow street lamp,
One pusher has been shot
Thru the throat
Big headlines in a flood:
WE DRINK EACH OTHER'S BLOOD
& CALL IT THOUGHT.
All of us are outsiders.

The Authentic Ship

Elizabeth Schultz

Though I am deep inland,
the grass off the highway,
the only sea, lifting wave
on wave to its long horizon,
ships move toward that line.
They sail through surging
water, spindrift flying. Lifted
on swells, they dip, sliding
down breakers, dissolving
into heaving turquoise water,
details of rigging and plank,
captain and crew liquefied.

But because I've trod
the *Morgan*'s deck, watched
her 19 sails unfurl, explored
her blubber room, because
I know her live oak keel
steadies her, she becomes
precise in word and paint.
With the barbaric *Pequod*,
Ryder's moonlit vessels,
Turner's whale ships, spewing
gore into a blood red dawn,
the *Morgan* now looms and
moves across the canvas
of my mind, sails billowing.

The Night Rockwell Kent Showed Me His Etchings

Alice Wolf Gilborn

He called this painting "Adirondacks" but it could be
anywhere, weathered buildings, wireless posts
against a fallow field, mountains rising darkly—
Empty homesteads strewn across the plains, hosts
to owls and spiders—these shells of former
lives ghosted my childhood. Landlocked
I pondered more exotic scenes.

Raw turbulence of mighty oceans is what I dreamed
at fourteen reading that black book, the whale's huge snout
streaming from the cover's depths. Every night I sailed
a restless sea aboard the *Pequod*, Ishmael, witness to it all:
Captain Ahab's mad pursuit of Moby Dick, the great whale
breached, transcendent, snapping boats in his jaws
smashing ships with his tail, diving finally as the sea
swept over, his tormentor lashed forever to his white
leviathan side. The book is gone but not the whale. Kent's
apotheosis leaps from the froth of Melville's wild
imaginings, etched a lifetime on my mind.

Later on a Massachusetts shore I watched the flat deceptive
sea and dug my heels into the sand, dwarfed and ignorant,
as when I met the man himself, Kent at Asgaard, images
of Moby Dick maneuvering his walls. From a drawer he
pulled proofs, spread them for inspection, larger than
the drawings I remembered. Freed from their
wordy element, they lay profoundly still
beached at last on Adirondack soil.

The hand that drew the ocean drew the land. I see it
in the mountains heaving toward the sky, motion
arrested, clouds roiling to a storm. Into this bleak
scenario slides light, washes mountain, house
barn, seeps into fields, into the earth itself
where underneath the ocean lies in wait
and all the great beasts swim.

Bone

Rick Mitchell

With a nod to Jasper Johns's *Ventriloquist*

Ahab stands at the mast, ranting invective against the wind;
his left-leg a whale-bone prosthesis pivoting in its notch on-deck.
The creaking of bone on oak soothing and haunting the ship
like the sullen rattle of an unseen snake in overgrown grass.
At his desk, Ahab daydreams, wriggles his left toes, scratches his left knee,
but as he swats a mosquito from his left calf, he's
jolted from his dream as his hand strikes unfeeling bone.

Ahab hobbles out onto the dark deck, alone with the sea.
No breeze but the ship glides along,
lured by the phantom whale.
While leaning against the bulwarks,
searching the surface, whale-bone between flesh and oak,
Ahab's a bearded conduit for Tragicall Nature;
shards of current shoot out from the gold doubloon on the mast.
Omens, presentiments charge through human sinew,
shoot through wood/world/oceanic membrane
as the past flits up for an ungraspable second
illuminating invisible whiteness impervious to surface.

Within the frame:
painted copies of paper American flags
attached to a painting of a painted door
enhanced by *trompe l'oeil* technique: shadow on a white vase.
A black and white painting in the painting.
Representations of representations
riding the white whale.
Foreboding jaw wide open: tungsten steel teeth.
Massive might twisted, wound tight, ready to strike,
speaking through mists of mind and epistemic murk
that can only hope to glimpse yet never contain the vertical whale.

An image is unhinged by yet another image.
Ungraspable terror at the heart of the paint.
The whale, copied from Moser's woodcut,
copied from lithographs, words, the book *Moby-Dick*;
copied from Melville's life, whaling tales, encyclopedias, the Bible.
Everything a copy of a copy.

Voices thrown hither and thither by sources unknown.
Unwilled speech of free will that cannot be found or MEAN.
Till the whale comes towards us, open-mouthed,
raising the waves on all sides and
beating the sea before him into a foam.

Canticle In The Fish's Belly

Rachel Richardson

How to get to it:
    the heart within
the corset
    made of whalebone
and Parisian leaded satin,
        winter weight.

I can barely breathe.

Sun filters from high windows
    into this dark-paneled room

where my sisters help me step
into the skirt,
        our grandmother's grandmother's
sent-for dress, its pinprick satin buttons
down my chest.
    We hook each hook
to hold the corset flush,
      to anchor
the bustle, as she did for her quiet
February wedding,
    snow covering the steeple
of the Seamen's Bethel.

      Melville: *This, shipmates, is that other lesson:*

fasten the locks, hold the heart
within its watery chamber.
        When the seamstress slid
the bone into the bodice
    and pinned each
cut piece together,
      the satin stood upright
at the sewing table.
She could almost
    see it breathe.

I am swallowed
and swallowed whole. It outlasts
      all our vows.

Whale, Cape Henlopen

William Orem

". . . all deep, earnest thinking is but the intrepid effort of the soul
to keep the open independence of her sea; while the wildest winds
of heaven and earth conspire to cast her of the treacherous, slavish shore."
    Moby-Dick, Chapter 23, "The Lee Shore"

By afternoon the sky was sooty, looming
        rain.
The broad Atlantic blew and turned
        and blew again.

And here it lay,

        slung up by some green wave
                and muttered over by approving crabs.

The meat was cleaned but recent.
                Living bone,

still pliant blue. An outraged mess
of gulls
                exploded off the glistering sand.

We still could see

 the gentle rest of hip in spine,
 a treasury of scattered vertebrae.

And something of the jaw, wherein
                        they say the music lies—

that long, expressive arc,

like us, that sings.

Calling Names: Margin Notes

Everett Hoagland

for Michael S. Harper,
who said, "When's the last time
you read Moby-Dick?
It's a labour of love."

Me?
I Love South Sea, African and Indian
women. *Fawns unsophisticated as leopardesses;*
loving as doves. Malintzin. Pocahontas. Maimiti.
Semen's Bethel.

The World is a treble-crown-knot.
I love to sail forbidden seas,
and land on barbarous coasts

My seed is as the *dust*
of the earth. . . if you can
number the dust of the earth
then
shall my seed also be numbered,

these are the sons of Ishmael,
and these are their names—
Who ain't a slave?

Cockades: mulatto, mestizo, eurasian.

Bloodknots: Blackwall hitch, reef knot,
                  clove hitch, Turk's head
                  granny knot.
Empire is macrame: Knot-in-and-out-knot,
          jamming knot.

I.
Call me Tashtego:
. . . a white horse, and he that set
on him had a bow;
and a crown
and he went forth conquering and to
conquer.

We saw the white horse and man as one
being,
our religion *giving the white man ideal*
mastership
over every dusky tribe. . .
Who ain't a slave?

II.
These tattoos are scrimshaw on
faith is my
marrow

Who ain't a slave?
My archipelago is now a pox.
My volcanic island,
a chancre,
the sea a missionary. It has
blue-green eyes. Night's white stare
gives it white skin.
I eat rotten fish and stale loaves.

Who ain't a slave?
Call me Queequeg

III.
Slave?
Always calling names.
Always calling *me* Ahab.
Projection is a bowsprit.
I am Paggoo. We Shall Overcome.

. . . to him that overcometh will
I give to eat of the hidden manna,
and will give him a white stone,
and in the stone a new name
written
which no man knoweth
saving he that receiveth it . . . NIGGER

Sequid vuestro jefe . . .
Always calling me out of my name.

Celestino: was a bowsprit.
I love to sail the forbidden seas
and land on buxom figure-heads,
the cliffs of Dover,

the same snowy mantle
round
our phantoms:
all ghosts rising in a milk-white fog.
the supernaturalism of this hue.
it shadows forth the heartless voids
and immensities of the universe . . .

The thought of annihilation
is not a color
so much as a visible absence
of color and
the concrete of all colors.

The Man Who Killed A Shadow:
the wretched infidel
gazes himself blind at
the monumental white shroud
that wraps all the prospect around him.

Wonder ye then at the fiery hunt

for the Wright whale
who ain't a slave?

when beholding the
white depth
of the Milky Way
I am drawn toward the closing
vortex . . . a creamy pool . . . forbidden seas

I love to sail forbidden seas
and land on barbarous coasts.

At the nadir. *Sequid vuestro jefe . . .*
Call me *Ixion.* Who ain't a slave

at
that vital centre?

IV.
Black bubble upward burst
the blues
no coffin saves me. Buoy:
the black bubble blues
the black bubble blues

Who ain't a slave? Atufal. Francesco. Babo.

Call me Babo
Call me Babo

On Johnny Cake Hill: A Sonic Vision

Everett Hoagland

I leave the hollow rib cage
of the whale's skeleton
in the museum on Johnny Cake Hill.

My own echoing footsteps
break the silence throbbing on
my ear drums.

Outside the doleful foghorn's pulsing
wails roll up from the waterfront
with the regularity of ocean waves. There is a break-
down by the curb of the quaintly re-cobbled
stoned street.

I assist a tourist, owner
of an old, fish-tailed, white Cadillac
that is overheated, spouting steam,
parked on the other side

of the headlong road a whole nation has
taken to Profits Point. The owner
complains about his energy-eating car
but brags,

"It's got a smooth transmission.
Listen to . . . "
the mechanical melody,
a whale's song modulated,
the desperate sonar of an endangered
species.

The unseen stream of sperm whale oil*
transmits a message. The whale's
sonic vision bounces off my soul's
ear. I hear blues: the desperate sonar

of an endangered species floats up
from the bandstands and jukeboxes
of waterfront cafes.

A palpable truth rises from these
sea-green blues like ambergris,
like Queequeg's coffin.
As we push the car to
the Whaling City Shell station,

the whole world is held fast
to my ear, like a sea shell,
in which I hear dying seas
and the extinction of singing things,
including us, in the cash register's

sounds, the mechanics of modulation.

---

* *Until relatively recent, some automatic transmission fluid contained oil derived from
sperm whales.*

Ishmael, or The Orphan

Dan Beachy-Quick

Before the God-bullied hull, call me—
Before the God-bullied hull buckles, before

The red flag unfurled on water bucks and drowns,
Before the sky-hawk dives down, before

The nail drives through the sky-hawk's red-wing—
Call me
              the nail driven through the wing
And call me the wing driven through.
A board
On water is buoyant, I know: I cling to wood—
A dictionary buckles and drowns. I know

I do not drown: I'm abridged, afloat, call me—

Sir, when my book arrives, when each page
You've untied lets go the breath it held
That was my breath, then breath will not be mine—
I think I'll know. I know when doors open
I mean to keep closed: study-door, desk-drawer.
My wife found the key I hid beneath the fern.
My pens she did not touch. She did not touch
The hundred pages I left blank to fill other days.
She took the cracked compass I keep for luck
(the needle's sharp, but stuck), took my green-glass
Ink-pot, and centering the compass on my desk,
Poured out each dark drop of ink until ink
Seeped through cracked glass and left the compass
Ink-full. The gold needle loosened, floated: a line.

Bent back, I am taking you inside my head
Turning back. Ahab bent

The needle that refused *North*
              back to a magnet's tow—
Did, Ahab did, after
The needle's faith answered our question: *No.*

How do you point at a horizon? Ask me. I know.
Needle out your arm: close eyes:

And turn in a circle. Inscribe a zero on the wood-deck—
The Equator on zero
              latitudes lies. That is the truth, I know

Sir, what name that bay a last page carves
Out of no shore: *ice? glacier? greenland?*
strand, shoal-of-white-sand? an arctic-calm?
How live, Sir, there—where I've been sailing?
Let me list for you, the cargo in my hold:
A brush, a mirror gilt-in-gold, a gold strand
Of wife's hair, a dirty plate, a sink with no water,
A white-sheeted bed, a finger with a ring
That the ring hates. Sir, these bound pages
Are bound for you. I've a compass
Full of ink. I see I need repair, plank
By plank, my boat, while ocean-bound, while afloat.

     I'm
     Orphan, Ishmael, Equator-Line:

     A man alone equals the wave before it crests,
     Wave, before crest, equals the needle turning,
     Needle turning equals the flinch of a hawk-wing,
     A hawk-wing's flinch is heaven turning

     Away. Men swallow water

Sir, I meant not to be so much myself
As I am. I meant to keep my mouth closed
When wife asked, "Should I go?" and I said: "Go."
Bow-of-the-bed, empty bow. I'm captain,
I guess, now. I fold the blank sheet back
Each morning. There's a page I mean to read.
No hand wrote it. It's white. It hides white
Inside another page of white. How, Sir—
Open a page inside a page? How, Sir, do you
Read the page that was written so you could not
Read it. I know, I think I know. You sleep,
Or step, or slip beneath the surface of the bed
And learn to breathe as paper breathes: with other's breath.

     And then water swallows men. A grave-magnet
     Pulls them down. Fathom me—

     Editor, fathom me. I am a known depth. I'm a
     Definition easy: a man, a mortal man,

     A man with five needles on each hand
     Pointing heavenward. Heed me. I'm lost.

Whale-line: allochthony

Kylan Rice

friend through ruin enter
        through this *long vatican*   of alcoves, entries, archways
        through what you think
an apex is is where
once there was   a gap between the ribs: a breadth that meant
                breath that meant
spume that made seethe the ocean made seethe the mind that seeds see
      here
      is that green
        prairie *where our children's grand-children will go*
        for bread here is that breadth with which we make do
for sea
      I think of you now
when I hear
      this word   *children*, think of your way of saying it
        think of when you said I am not a man I am
a father,
where a father is   who cares, where care is   an eclipse, a pupil   all iris,
nowhere   to enter, where to enter   is to leave; where care is
        the eye forgetting
it takes in
through a hole
that grows   greedy as the light   leaves (late, consumptive)—
        a daughter-swallowed pip
that reflex breadth that otherwise   is apex, transom, lintel
        enter;

        advance through
this material, I have been trying to learn   all there is to know
about advanced material, additive
      manufacturing, powder markets, powdered carbon alloy steel
      for use in sintering, in precision, in printing

a part, whole and unto
itself, as additive as   tissue is, less   subtractive, shorn, carpentered, lathed, god
knows what a lathe is, as for us   what a lathe is is what it makes
                                        and doesn't stand
for anything; what our work is is   the object and the thought at once, not separate, soldered,
bolted, bridge, marvel of reach   across an inclusion   of sea, a reach that is in essence
                                                                line and lines
can be plucked, reach   a resonant frequency, trough and crest, and what is a wave
but collapse, but shoring, but being   regurgitated back

                                        friend (can I call you
that?) you start with a door
that is shut, you start with a hull
that is sealed
that plows that breadth   where breath was (yours), where now
                                        mine is, miner, sub-sub   -sub
                                        burrower   for a ground, for a
                                        mineral bed, a rime
of salt but not   of the sea, not the scent from the seethe   of the break, instead the salt
from the sweat of your brow, sweat-sintering
                                        myself a ground from that, grinding, powdering
down to print into tissue, cell
                        after cell after cell

                                        after you

Whale-line: built environment

Kylan Rice

again I find myself
                    as I did all winter
before another cluster
                    of sugar beet silos, plus nearby an obelisk, smoke
                    stack of a lumber plant, universal forest products—
            the teacher of my teacher asking too *the plants*
            to give me my small   identity, windsor, co, adjacent too to
                                        chimney park the swimming pool

again I find myself facing thinking

                            scale, storage, this is a sphinx, pyramid
                            but of the plains, find myself a lip
                            at a cluster, density
                            of motif, abundance of, of here
                            architectural, here
                            vegetable, now zoo
                            -morphic, undoing from structure
                                    into ornament, flower, then back
            into stem, wasp   into orchid into wasp what is an identity

but vector, merger, lip
                    verging on a brimming, blushful   hippocrene, the pool horse-hoof-struck,
striker sprung from blood of the gorgon, bronze
gore cast all at once by cellini his *perseus,* source
                                of poetry, wine, exhaustion, beauty, *impetuous*
                                pour poured out of re-forged platters, porringers,
                                pewter cups, once a cup now this
                                quick of the elbow holding me out
                                too, bear me out too *if I shall touch   that*
                                workman's arm with some ethereal light, if I shall
                                touch
                                        lightly, glory
                                        the wound the workman
                                        makes, the quiver
of legs, whale-wounded, wound that lives   past healing, is still springing, surplus, bronze as the blood is,
but given, not handed   me myself, also these   legs lathed for me, leg that is

an arrow, a leaving a leaving   a never arriving,   a transfer, trans-
                                            fusion, pure pour, whelming over,
over-
plus, plus   obelisk, silo, plus what is in the silo, grain density, the trans-
                                    verse weight of it

Razo—On the Nature of the Book as the Nature of the Whale

Dan Beachy-Quick

Editor,

Teeth and pages and the whale are white.
I am white, and the white of the eye
Is the eye's blindness, that *black-hollow*, the *pupil*,
Is sight. Do you see how a book changes
Its white nature? A first page turns away
From an unread, ocean's depth. Chapters?
How blackly we see our fingers fold down
A page on the dark shore. A last page
Crests, spills over, a white foam on land—
We remember the ocean as drowned men
Remember the shore. But, Sir—
                                        I differ here:
This book I'm reading is a
Book that to mark a page is as hard
As folding in half an ocean-wave to know—
In latitudes—where you are. Where am I?
In *A Glossed Concordance*
Of the Sea Language
                in Melville's Novels
I learn a fact. Previous books the author filled
With *bay, beach, shore, isles, ports*—
This book is written *castaway, depth* and *deep, fathomless,*
Flooded and *unshored*, without a
Port Authority. I find myself adrift
In middle chapters; I practice holding breath—.
To sound is to dive down. A whale's
Deepest sounding ends with inspiration's
Need. I've read one book three times, Sir—
With Pip, afloat on the flat surface
Above the white whale's rising, God omnipotent,
I'm scared to breathe and not to.

I am not the Whale

Faith St. John

I used to think
that I could be the whale

but no one came looking for me.

There I was
spending time alone at the bottom
and the phone never rang.

When I surfaced
I could see the ships surrounding other warm bodies
their words harpoon ready.

I knew then that I was not the subject
of either their regard or their aggression

and I was free to dive
and surface
and dive again.

The Chase—Third Day

Tim Wood

PROSECUTION

Etymology

(Supplied by Collins English Dictionary—
complete & unabridged 2012 digital edition.)

PROSECUTION [pros-i-kyoo-shuh n]. The following up of something undertaken or begun, usually to its completion. < Late Latin prōsecūtiōn (stem of prōsecūtiō) a following up. See prosecute, -ion n. 1560s, "action of pursuing," from Middle French prosecution (late 13 c.) and directly from Late Latin prosecutionem (nominativeprosecutio) "a following," noun of action from past participle stem of prosequi (see prosecute).

P E R U P I C T U R E
S P I N E P I N T P I
T E O U S P O E T P O
I N T P O O R P O R E
P O R T P O R T I O N
P O S T P O S T U R E
P O T P O T I O N P O
U N C E P O U R P R E
C I O U S P R I C E P
R O N E P R O P O S E
P R O S E P U R E P U
R S E P U R S U E P U
T R E C O U N T R I O
T R I P E R I P T R O
O T R O P E R O S E R
O T R O U T I N E R U
I N R U N R U S T O N
C E O N E O U N C E O
U S T O U T S C E N T
S C O O T S C O R E S
C O R N S E C T I O N
S E C U R E S E N O R
S I R S I T S N O R E

```
S   O   N   S   O   R   E   S   O   R   T
S   O   U   R   C   E   S   P   I   C   E
S   P   I   N   E   S   P   I   T   S   P
I   T   E   S   P   O   O   N   S   P   O
T   S   P   O   U   T   S   P   R   O   U
T   S   P   U   R   N   S   T   I   R   S
T   O   I   C   S   T   O   O   P   S   T
O   P   S   T   R   U   T   S   T   U   N
S   T   U   P   O   R   S   U   C   T   I
O   N   S   U   I   T   S   U   N   E   R
U   P   T   I   O   N   C   E   N   T   C
I   T   E   C   I   T   I   E   S   C   O
I   N   C   O   N   E   S   C   O   N   S
P   I   R   E   C   O   O   P   E   R   C
O   P   I   E   S   C   O   R   N   C   O
R   P   S   E   C   O   U   N   T   E   R
S   C   O   U   N   T   R   I   E   S   C
O   U   R   S   E   C   O   U   R   T   C
O   U   S   I   N   C   R   E   P   T   C
R   I   E   S   C   R   O   N   I   E   S
C   R   U   E   T   C   U   E   C   U   P
C   U   R   E   C   U   R   I   O   S   C
U   R   I   O   U   S   C   U   R   S   E
```

```
C  U  T  U  N  I  T  U  P  O  N
U  S  E  R  T  I  P  S  T  O  E
T  O  N  I  C  T  O  P  T  O  R
S  O  T  R  I  E  S  T  R  I  O
T  R  I  P  T  R  O  O  P  S  T
R  O  P  I  C  T  R  U  C  E  T
U  N  I  C  T  U  N  S  T  U  R
N  I  C  E  I  N  S  E  C  T  I
R  O  N  O  P  E  N  O  P  I  N
E  O  R  I  E  N  T  N  E  S  T
N  E  T  S  N  I  C  E  N  O  O
S  E  N  O  S  E  N  O  T  N  O
T  I  C  E  S  N  U  R  S  E  N
   U        T        S
```

A Rose Sea

Tim Wood

A R O S E A R O S E A

R O S E A R O S E A R

O S E A R O S E A R O

S E A R O S E A R O S

E A R O S E A R O S E

A R O S E A R I S E S

straight up, leaps thy apotheosis!

White Whale

Jeffrey Yang

Round and round we wheel
around the White Whale
in a braided cord
of good and evil,
     till self's
freed
from ego.

From *Debths*

Susan Howe

These tallied scraps float
like glass skiffs quietly for
love or pity and all that

What an idea in such a time
as ours Pip among Pleiads

Acknowledgments

Dan Beachy-Quick's poems appeared in *Spell* (Ahsahta Press, 2004).

Anthony Caleshu's "Whale Watching" appeared in *Of Whales: in Print, in Paint, in Sea, in Stars, in Coin, in House, in Margins* (Salt, 2010).

Jessica Cuello's "Chapter 31: Queen Mab," "Chapter 36: The Quarter-Deck," "Chapter 44: The Chart," and "Chapter 92: Ambergris" appeared in *Hunt* (The Word Works, 2017).

Alice Wolf Gilborn's "The Night Rockwell Kent Showed Me His Etchings" appeared in *Taking Root*. Copyright © 2012 by Alice Wolf Gilborn. Reprinted with permission of The Permissions Company, Inc., on behalf of Finishing Line Press, www.finishinglinepress.com.

Michalle Gould's "Enveloped in whale-lines" appeared in *The Toast* (February 3, 2015).

Everett Hoagland's "On Johnny Cake Hill: A Sonic Vision" appeared in *This City and Other Poems* (Spinner Publications, 1999).

Everett Hoagland's "Calling Names: Margin Notes" appeared in *Scrimshaw* (Patmos Press, 1976).

Susan Howe's poem, "These tallied scraps float...," is from *Debths*, copyright © 2013, 2014, 2015, 2016, 2017. Reprinted by permission of New Directions Publishing Corp.

Ivan Klein's "Prelude" and "Ishmael" appeared in *Toward Melville: Poems from the Life and Work of Herman Melville* (New Feral Press, 2018).

Danelle Lejeune, "Etymology of Whale-Fish and Grace" from *Landlocked: Etymology of Whale-Fish and Grace*. Copyright © 2017 by Danelle Lejeune. Reprinted with the permission of The Permissions Company, Inc., on behalf of Finishing Line Press, www.finishinglinepress.com.

Deborah Meadows's "Chapter 68" and "Chapter 69" appeared in the Tinfish Press chapbook (Kane'ohe, Hawaii, 2003), titled *The 60's and 70's: from The Theory of Subjectivity in Moby-Dick*, and was subsequently included in *Translation, the bass accompaniment: Selected Poems* (Shearsman Press, 2013).

Rick Mitchell's "Bone" appeared in *Leviathan*, 8.1, March (2006), 85 and 87. The Johns Hopkins University Press and the Melville Society. Reprinted with permission of Johns Hopkins University Press.

William Orem's "Whale, Cape Henlopen" appeared in *Color Wheel* and was subsequently printed in *Our Purpose in Speaking* (MSU Press, 2018).

Louis Phillips "Six Poems from *Bulkington*" were excerpted from *Bulkington* (Hollow Spring Press, 1981) to be included in *Leviathan* (5.1, March 2003).

Diane Raptosh's "ix.)" appeared under the title "Selections from The Zygote Epistles" in *Leviathan*, 19.3, October (2017), 105-118. © The Johns Hopkins University Press and Melville Society. Reprinted with permission of Johns Hopkins University Press.

Rachel Richardson, "Of Whales in Paint; in Teeth; in Wood; in Sheet-Iron; in Stone; in Mountains; in Stars," "A Brief History of the Whale Fishery" and "Canticle in the Fish's Belly" from *Hundred-Year Wave*. Copyright © 2016 by Rachel Richardson. Reprinted with the permission of The Permissions Company, Inc., on behalf of Carnegie Mellon University Press, www.cmu.edu/universitypress.

Laurie Robertson-Lorant's "Melville in the Enchanted Nursery" appeared in *The Man Who Lived Among the Cannibals: Poems in the Voice of Herman Melville* (Spinner Publications, 2005).

Elizabeth Schultz's "The *Morgan* on Stellwagon Bank" appeared in Leviathan (17.1, March 2015). This poem and her other poems here appeared in *Ishmael on the* Morgan (self-published, 2015).

Douglas Storm's "Tablets" appeared in *Leviathan*, 15.1, March (2013), 82-84. © The Johns Hopkins University Press and Melville Society. Reprinted with permission of Johns Hopkins University Press.

John Struloeff's "As My Uncle Rides an Exercise Bike at the Rec Center, He Tries to Explain *Moby-Dick* to the Man Riding Beside Him" appeared in *Prairie Schooner* (80.4, Winter 2006).

Jeffrey Yang's "White Whale" appeared in, *An Aquarium*. Copyright 2008 by Jeffrey Yang. Reprinted with permission of The Permissions Company, Inc., on behalf of Finishing Line Press, www.finishinglinepress.com.

Biographical Information

Devon Balwit lives in Portland, Oregon, and has written chapbooks inspired by *Moby-Dick*, *Wise Blood*, and *In Search of Lost Time*, among others.

Dan Beachy-Quick teaches at Colorado State University and is the author of *Gentlessness* (Tupelo Press, 2015), *Of Silence and Song* (Milkweed Editions, 2017), and *Variations on Dawn and Dusk* (forthcoming).

Anthony Caleshu teaches at the University of Plymouth, UK. He is the author of *A Dynamic Exchange Between Us* (Shearsman, 2019), *The Victor Poems* (Shearsman, 2015), and *Of Whales: in Print, in Paint, in Sea, in Stars, in Coin, in House, in Margins* (Salt, 2010).

Sylvia Cavanaugh teaches high school cultural studies in Sheboygan, Wisconsin. A Pushcart Prize nominee, her chapbooks include *Staring Through My Eyes* (Finishing Line Press, 2014) and *Angular Embrace* (Kelsay Books, 2018).

Jessica Cuello lives in Syracuse, New York, and is the author of *Hunt* (Word Works, 2017) and *Pricking* (Tiger Bark Press, 2016).

Adam Day lives in Louisville, Kentucky. His books include *Left-Handed Wolf* (LSU Press, forthcoming, 2020) and *Model of a City in Civil War* (Sarabande Books, 2015). He is also the editor of the anthology, *Divine Orphans of the Poetic Project*, forthcoming from 1913 Press.

Mira Dougherty-Johnson lives in East Hampton, New York. Her work has appeared in *Fourth Genre*, *The Southeast Review*, and *Tupelo Quarterly*.

Waldo Gemio lives in London, U.K. His short story, "The Company or Cannibals," was anthologized in *Premonitions: Causes for Alarm* (Pigasus Press, 2008) as well as Dark Recesses Press. His poetry has appeared in *Other Poetry*, *Chronogram*, *Orbis*, and other venues.

Alice Wolf Gilborn lives in East Dorset, Vermont. She is the author of *What Do You Do with a Kinkajou?* (J. B. Lippincott, 1976; 2nd rev. edition, The Blueline Press, 2017), *Taking Root* (Finishing Line Press, 2012), and *Out of the Blue: Blueline Essays 1979–1989* (Potsdam College Press, 2013).

Michalle Gould lives in Los Angeles. She is the author of *Resurrection Party* (Silver Birch Press, 2014). Her short story "The Garden of Evil" won the 2017 Moment Magazine-Karma Foundation Short Fiction Contest. Her poem, "How Not to Need Resurrection," was adapted into a short film for the sixth season of Motionpoems.

Everett Hoagland is an emeritus professor of English at the University of Massachusetts Dartmouth. His work has appeared in numerous anthologies and several books, including, . . . Here. . . : *New and Selected Poems* (Leapfrog Press, 2002) and *Encounters: Poems about Race, Ethnicity, and Identity* (Skinner House, 2011).

Susan Howe has published thirteen books with New Directions, including *Debths* (2017).

David Kann is professor emeritus teaching at California Polytechnic State University, San Luis Obispo. He is the author of two chapbooks: *The Language of the Farm*, winner of the "Our Wish for Blue" contest of Five Oaks Press, and *At Fernald School* (Finishing Line Press).

Ivan Klein lives in Manhattan. His publications include *Toward Melville* (New Feral Press), *Some Paintings by Koho & A Flower of My Own* (Sisyphus Press), and *Alternatives To Silence* (Starfire Press).

Jim LaVilla-Havelin lives in Lytle, Texas. The coordinator of National Poetry Month activities in San Antonio and the *San Antonio* and *Houston Express News* Poetry Editor, he is a teacher, critic, and community arts activist. The author of five books of poems, including *WEST, poems of a place* (Wings Press, 2017), his works have been included in in numerous anthologies, most recently: *Visiting Bob: Poems Inspired by the Life and Work of Bob Dylan* (New Rivers Press, 2018) and *The Enchantment of the Ordinary* (Mutabilis Press, 2019).

Danelle Lejeune lives near Savannah, Georgia, where she is the assistant director of the Ossabaw Island Writers Retreat. She also teaches for Georgia Southern University. Her work has been published in *Whale Road Review*, *Glass*, and *Nottingham Review*.

Robert McGowan is a publisher with St. Clair Press. His publications include *A Year on The River* (2011), *Marsha*, a children's book (2014), and poems in the *Oakland Journal* (Winter, 2008).

Deborah Meadows lives in Los Angeles and is an emerita faculty from California State Polytechnic University. She is the author of *Lecture Notes: A duration poem in twelve parts* (BlazeVOX Books, 2018), *The Demotion of Pluto: Poems and Plays* (BlazeVOX Books, 2017), and, as part of her *Moby-Dick* poetry project, *Itinerant Men* (Krupskaya Press, 2004).

Rick Mitchell, who spent time at sea working on cruise ships, is currently a land-locked playwright, poet, and performance scholar. His books include *Disaster Capitalism; Or Money Can't Buy You Love, The Composition of Herman Melville, Ventriloquist,* and *Brecht in L.A.,* and he's the editor of *Experimental O'Neill.* Mitchell is Professor of English at California State University, Northridge.

Rajiv Mohabir, author of *The Cowherd's Son* (Tupelo Press, 2017) and *The Taxidermist's Cut* (Four Way Books, 2016), is currently an Assistant Professor in Poetry at Auburn University.

William Orem lives outside Boston, and is a Senior Writer-in-Residence at Emerson College. His first collection of poems, *Our Purpose in Speaking,* won the Wheelbarrow Books Poetry Prize from MSU Press. His novel, *Miss Lucy,* about the life of Bram Stoker, published in 2019, won the Gival Press Novel Award.

Louis Phillips is a Humanities Professor at the School of Visual Arts in New York City. His most recent publications are *The Domain of Small Mercies: New and Selected Poems 2* (1963-2015), published by Pleasure Boat Studio; *Celebrations & Bewilderments* (World Audience Books, 2018); and *Dial M for Miscellany* (a collection of his Mystery Scene Magazine columns).

Patrick Pritchett is Associate Professor of English at Hunan Normal University, Changsha, China. His most recent books of poetry are *Song X* and *Orphic Noise.*

Diane Raptosh teaches literature and creative writing at the College of Idaho, where she also runs the program in criminal justice studies. Her previous publications include *American Amnesiac* (Etruscan Press, 2013), *Human Directional* (Etruscan Press, 2016), and *Parents from a Different Alphabet* (Guernica Editions, 2008). Her forthcoming book, *Dear Z: The Zygote Epistles* (Etruscan Press, 2020), will feature poems about *Moby-Dick.*

Kylan Rice lives in North Carolina. His poetry and prose has been published in *Tupelo Quarterly, Denver Quarterly, West Branch, Kenyon Review,* and elsewhere.

Rachel Richardson is the author of two books of poetry, *Hundred-Year Wave* (2016) and *Copperhead* (2011), both in the Carnegie Mellon Poetry Series. A recipient of Stegner and NEA Fellowships, she teaches in the MFA program at the University of San Francisco and co-directs the community literary center, Left Margin LIT, in Berkeley, California.

Laurie Robertson-Lorant, who has taught at University of Massachusetts Dartmouth, MIT, and Bridgewater State University, is the author of *Melville: A Biography* (1996) and *The Man Who Lived Among the Cannibals: In the Voice of Herman Melville* (2005). At present, she is preparing an updated, re-titled edition of her Melville biography. Her poetry has received several awards.

Jeff Saperstein lives in the New River Valley of southwestern Virginia. After thirty years of teaching English at Radford University, he retired in 2015. His poem, "Melville's Second Son," appeared in *Main Street Rag* in 2014. He won first prize for his poem "The Minimalist" (*Common Ground Review,* 2011).

Elizabeth Schultz's *"Unpainted to the Last":* Moby-Dick *and American Art,* and her essay, "The New Art of *Moby-Dick*" (Leviathan, 2019), reflect her recognition of the impact of Melville's novel on art and culture. She has also published five books of poetry, a collection of short stories, a memoir, and a collection of nature essays.

Nicholas Spengler lives in Oxford, U.K. The author of *Your Voice in Half-Light* (Honeybee Press, 2013), his poetry and prose have appeared in *The Café Review* and *The Salon: A Journal of Poetry & Fiction.*

Douglas Storm lives in Bloomington, Indiana. He is host and producer of Interchange, an interview program on community radio station WFHB, which focuses on arts, history, and politics. His poems appear in his poetry collection, *The Gulf of Folly* (Black Bomb Books, 2016).

John Struloeff is associate professor and director of creative writing at Pepperdine University in Malibu, California. His poems have appeared in *The Atlantic, The Southern Review,* and *Prairie Schooner.*

Faith St. John lives in Argyle, New York. She is president of the Drunk Poets Society of the Adirondacks. Her work has been included in the anthologies, *Paw Prints in Verse* (2017), and the *Ishka Bibble Book of Desire,* which is forthcoming.

Lee Upton is the writer-in-residence at Lafayette College. She is the author of *Visitations: Stories* and *Bottle the Bottles the Bottles the Bottles: Poems,* as well as *The Tao of Humiliation: Stories,* and other books.

Onyinye Miriam Uwolloh, from Lagos, Nigeria, is majoring in psychology with a minor in biological sciences at Northern Kentucky University. The poem in this volume is her first publication.

Tim Wood teaches at SUNY Nassau Community College. The author of *Otherwise Known as Home* (BlazeVOX, 2010) and *Notched Sunsets* (Atelos, 2016), he is co-editor of *The Hip Hop Reader* (Longman, 2008).

Jeffrey Yang is the author of poetry books, *An Aquarium, Vanishing-Line,* and *Hey, Marfa.* He lives in Beacon, New York.